"This is an imminently practical workbook that shows a variety of invaluable techniques to get centered, calm and organized. An effective and enjoyable guide to help you feel in charge of yourself"

Bessel van der Kolk, M.D. Renowned trauma expert, author & psychiatrist.

"Linda Curran has carefully and knowledgeably curated a practical, effective collection of interventions that actually work for trauma survivors. Any clinician committed to helping those suffering from posttraumatic stress needs to have these tools and resources to draw upon, because standard talk therapy, nine times out of ten, is simply not going to cut it. These exercises will."

Belleruth Naparstek, LISW author of *Invisible Heroes: Survivors of Trauma and How They Heal*

"Drawing from the whole spectrum of trauma-based therapies, Linda Curran has compiled a sampling of practical exercises designed to help therapists and their clients better navigate the mine field that trauma work can be and find the path to healing."

Richard Schwartz, Ph.D. author of *Internal Family Systems Therapy*

"Like all of Curran's work, 101 Trauma-Informed Interventions is thoughtful, engaging and practical. Her book provides an array of solid interventions drawn from the growing trauma literature. Both new and experienced therapists will enrich their clinical practices by reading this book. It should be part of every therapist's library."

Mike Dubi, Ed.D., LMHC President, International Association of Trauma Professionals

"*101 Trauma-Informed Interventions* provides an accessible functional "playbook" for therapists committed to the rehabilitation of the client with a trauma history. In a readable volume Curran integrates diverse approaches of treatment and emphasizes the unique role that trauma plays in mental health. Underlying this eclectic strategy is the common theme emphasizing that healing will only begin when the trauma related feelings embedded in the body are appreciated."

Stephen W. Porges, Ph.D. author of *The Polyvagal Theory*

"An interesting compendi... ... .ions that can be interwoven into any therapist's existing conceptual framework"

Louis Cozolino, Ph.D. Pepperdine University, and author of 5 books including the best-seller *The Neuroscience of Psychotherapy, Healing the Social Brain* (2nd edition)

"Linda Curran's unflagging energy and dedication to the healing of traumatized individuals has led to a voluminous, exciting, and comprehensive, *101 Trauma Informed Interventions*. This workbook provides a plethora of effective tools -- traditional as well as innovative -- that can be used in whole or as a part of a course of therapy and also as self-help. The variety of options offered goes a long way towards dispelling the (unfortunately) popular misconception that there are only a limited number of interventions that help people to recover from trauma. Survivors as well as therapists who have been frustrated by the rigidity of strict adherence to evidence based practice will be greatly relieved to find a wealth of useful strategies to experiment, evaluate, and sort into a personally tailored trauma recovery program. This workbook is a god-send for the trauma field, expanding the possibilities for recovery in a most generous way."

Babette Rothschild, MSW author of *The Body Remembers and 8 Keys to Safe Trauma Recovery*

"Branching from her outstanding manual Trauma Competency, expert therapist and author Linda Curran's *101 Trauma-Informed Interventions* delivers nearly 200 practical interventions for those who work with people with traumatic histories (nearly all of us).

Comprehensive in theory to application, the wealth of information in this book will expand the practice of both those new to and experienced in trauma work with interventions that integrate mind, body, and spirit in the healing process. Delivered with belief and expectancy in the context of a therapeutic alliance, these activities, exercises, and assignments will create safety, containment, and ultimately, transformation."

Lane D. Pederson, PsyD, LP, DBTC author of *The Expanded Dialectical Behavior Skills Training Manual: Practical DBT for Self-help and Individual & Group Treatment Settings* and *DBT Skills Training in Integrated Dual Disorder Treatment Settings*

101 TRAUMA-INFORMED INTERVENTIONS

Activities, Exercises and Assignments to Move the Client and Therapy Forward

by

Linda A. Curran
BCPC, LPC, CCDP, CAC-D

PESI
Publishing
& Media
www.pesipublishing.com

Copyright © 2013 by Linda Curran

Published by
PESI Publishing and Media
PESI, Inc.
3839 White Ave
Eau Claire, WI 54703

Printed in the United States of America

Cover Design: Amy Rubenzer
Edited by: Marietta Whittlesey & Bookmasters
Page Design: Bookmasters

ISBN: 978-1-93612-842-6

"The Past: Our cradle, not our prison; there is danger as well as appeal in its glamour. The past is for inspiration, not imitation, for continuation, not repetition."
~ Israel Zangwill

"However many holy words you read, however many you speak, what good will they do you if you do not act upon them?"
~ Buddha

May I gratefully acknowledge the support of my loving family, dear friends, esteemed colleagues, and my many, many truly unbelievably gracious mentors, which includes each one of my clients—past and present.

Words are inadequate to recount how you've blessed me.

*This book is dedicated to the memory of one of the kindest men
I've ever known, Tony Coladonato.*

You are loved always, and missed hourly.

Table of Contents

About the Author

Linda Curran, BCPC, LPC, CAACD, CCDP sought after national trainer, best-selling author on trauma and a film producer. Linda has trained thousands of mental health clinicians on trauma treatment across the country. She is President of Integrative Trauma, LLC, in Havertown, Pennsylvania. With advanced degrees in both clinical psychology and public health, Linda is a Board Certified, Licensed Professional Counselor; Certified Addiction Counselor Diplomate; Certified Co-Occurring Professional Diplomate; Certified Gestalt Therapist; Certified Hypnotherapist; Level II EMDR practitioner.

Author of *Trauma Competency: A Clinicians Guide* and international speaker on the treatment of trauma, Linda has developed, produced, and presents multi-media workshops on all aspects of psychological trauma. Latest projects include the completion of www.trauma101.com (an extensive trauma resource for clinicians and clients alike) and two video projects for *The Master Clinician Series: 1. Trauma Treatment: Psychotherapy for the 21st Century and 2. Power Therapies: EMDR and Beyond*. Linda continues to advocate for accessible, coherent, integrative trauma treatment for all those affected by trauma.

Introduction

In all honesty, I can't say that as a professional entering the mental health field I had not heard of the diagnosis **PTSD**, or post-traumatic stress disorder. I had. In fact, in graduate school I had heard of it twice: once within a required course on psychopathology and, then again, within a required course on the *Diagnostic and Statistical Manual of Mental Disorders* (DSM). Sadly, what neither of those courses required of me was that I learn what "**T**" was, all that "**T**" encompassed, how pervasive "**T**" was, both in the general and psychiatric populations, or how "**T**" appears to be present in almost all psychopathology and in nearly every psychological disorder catalogued in the DSM.

Perhaps you are thinking that somehow this makes sense. Way back then, the DSM was new; people knew very little about trauma; and modern brain imaging techniques—CT, FMRI, PET, and SPECT—were all still the stuff of science fiction. How could I have possibly been well-informed on a subject for which there was so little information? I was a product of my time. Right? Wrong. The iteration of the DSM that my class studied, DSM IV-TR, was published in 2000 and, in addition to earlier writings of Freud, Ferenczi, Kardiner, and Janet, a considerable amount of information regarding trauma had been gleaned and made available in *this century*. The following are a few of the highlights and trauma resources from the last two decades that most certainly would have proved helpful had I been pointed to them:

- In 1992, *Trauma and Recovery: The Aftermath of Violence—from Domestic Abuse to Political Terror* was published. Judith Lewis Herman, its author, wrote:

  > The responses to trauma are best understood as a spectrum of conditions rather than as a single disorder. They range from a brief stress reaction that gets better by itself and never qualifies for a diagnosis, to classic or simple post-traumatic stress disorder, to the complex syndrome of prolonged, repeated trauma.

  > In survivors of prolonged, repeated trauma, the symptom picture is often far more complex. Survivors of prolonged abuse develop characteristic personality changes, including deformations of relatedness and identity. Survivors of abuse in childhood develop similar problems with relationships and identity; in addition, they are particularly vulnerable to repeated harm, both self-inflicted and at the hands of others. The current formulation of post-traumatic stress disorder fails to capture either the protean symptomatic manifestations of prolonged, repeated trauma or the profound deformations of personality that occur in captivity. The syndrome that follows upon prolonged repeated trauma needs its own name. I propose to call it "complex post-traumatic stress disorder." (p. 119)

- In 1994, Bessel van der Kolk's seminal paper, "The Body Keeps the Score: Memory & the Evolving Psychobiology of Post-Traumatic Stress," was published in the *Harvard Review of Psychiatry*

- In 1996, Bessel van der Kolk's first book, *Traumatic Stress: The Effects of Overwhelming Experience on Mind, Body, and Society*, presents theory and research of trauma's lasting effects on an individual's biology, conceptions of the world, and psychological functioning; the neurobiological processes underlying PTSD symptomatology, traumatic memories, and dissociation; and the core components of effective clinical interventions.

- In 1997, Peter Levine's first book, *Waking the Tiger: Healing Trauma: The Innate Capacity to Transform Overwhelming Experiences,* presents a new and hopeful vision of trauma. Levine wrote:

> Trauma is perhaps the most avoided, ignored, belittled, denied, misunderstood, and untreated cause of human suffering. Although it is the source of tremendous distress and dysfunction, it is not an ailment or a disease, but the byproduct of an instinctively instigated, altered state of consciousness. We enter this altered state—let us call it "survival mode"—when we perceive that our lives are being threatened. If we are overwhelmed by the threat and are unable to successfully defend ourselves, we can become stuck in survival mode. This highly aroused state is designed solely to enable short-term defensive actions; but left untreated over time, it begins to form the symptoms of trauma. These symptoms can invade every aspect of our lives. Trauma is a basic rupture—loss of connection—to ourselves, our families, and the world. The loss, although enormous, is difficult to appreciate because it happens gradually. We adjust to these slight changes, sometimes without taking notice of them at all. Contrary to the view of psychiatric medicine—that trauma is basically untreatable and only marginally controllable by drugs—when treated thoroughly healing can lead not only to symptom reduction, but long-term transformation. (p. 23)

Unfortunately and unnecessarily, I, like so many others, entered the field without those resources. I was equipped only with a diploma, a solemn desire to help and a set of freshly honed cognitive behavioral therapy (CBT) skills that I had perfected in role-playing sessions with my fellow graduate students. It would take a month or two of working with actual clients before I noticed that, unlike my classmates, who were quite taken with my ability to explain a *thought record* in a practice session, my clients. . . .not so much. Nor should they have been, because they were getting no help from me.

It was about the same time that I began to truly grasp the degree, acuity, and severity of trauma—both acute and developmental—that each one of my clients had not only endured, but continued to endure and embody in the present. Back then, the one thing that I knew with certainty was that because I lacked the knowledge, information, and resources to be of any assistance to these people, they were screwed. Again. But this time they were not alone; we both felt *trapped*, we both felt *helpless,* and we both felt *overwhelmed*.

At that point, one of two things usually happens. Either we blame the client or we blame ourselves. The first gives rise to a terrible therapist; the second, a soon-to-be burned out, a.k.a. *former,* therapist. Okay, maybe it's not quite that simple or predictable. For me, what came was a galvanizing realization that each of my clients—stronger, more courageous versions of myself— were sitting across from me, looking at and to me, wordlessly insisting that I become a better person and a better therapist. I complied because each one so obviously deserved a better person and a better therapist than I was. Years later I discovered that somebody had anonymously put words to what I had only vaguely known:

> *They are survivors. If you don't have respect for their strength, you can't be of any help. It's a privilege that they let you in—there's no reason they should trust you, none. You can't know their*

terror. It's your worst nightmare come true, a nightmare from which you can never awaken. It's unrelenting. There has been no safety: no one, no time, nothing—all was tainted. Hope was obliterated time and time again. That they are in our office is in itself a supreme act of valor.

Last year, I had the great fortune and honor of interviewing many of the icons in field of traumatic stress, including Dr. Bessel van der Kolk. His impassioned plea to psychotherapists was incredibly moving and bears repeating: "What I'd like to say is that good trauma work is like very fine neurosurgery. It is extremely skilled work. And good intentions and warm feelings do not substitute for really becoming very good at what you do."

It is my hope that this book serves not only as a concrete collection of trauma-informed interventions, but as an inspiration for you to continue "becoming very good at what you do."

About the Book

First, the title is a marketing ploy: at last count there were more than 190 interventions. However, *101* has not only that Dalmatian-like familiarity that I think will sell better, it just so happens to be the name of my website: **www.trauma101.com**. So, please visit.

Secondly, for your convenience, we have established a dedicated website to download all the worksheets and exercises. This gives you a choice to photocopy from the book or printing. The exercises will all be labeled with the corresponding titles and pages.

go.pesi.com/trauma101

Finally, with regard to the interventions themselves: in my personal and professional development, as both client and clinician, I have witnessed and/or experienced each of these interventions. I was—and continue to be—amazed by their power. Each one addresses some aspect of trauma and can be used with individuals, groups and couples. (Where appropriate, distinctions regarding population are noted.) Clinicians should encourage clients to remain present and mindful throughout the action phase of each intervention, and reflective throughout its processing phase. Without such a stance, they're really just activities.

Adult Attachment Patterns

To capture a broad-stroke depiction of attachment, Mary Main and her colleagues developed a semistructured interview about childhood attachment relationships and the meaning the individual *currently gives to those past relational experiences.* The individuals account is examined for material that is explicitly expressed by the individual and for material that appears out of the interviewee's awareness (e.g., apparent incoherence and inconsistencies of dialogue) with the aim of assessing the unconscious elements of the attachment relationship.

Scoring is based upon:

(a) descriptions of childhood experiences

(b) language used in the interview

(c) ability to give an integrated, believable account of experiences and their meaning

The language and conversation style used is considered to reflect the state of mind of the interviewee with respect to attachment. The Adult Attachment Inventory (AAI) is then scored from the transcript using scales that characterize childhood experience with each parent as loving, rejecting, neglecting, involving, or pressuring. Other scales assess conversational style, overall coherence of transcript and of thought, idealization, active anger, fear of loss, metacognitive monitoring, and passivity of speech. Scale scores are then used to assign the adult to one of three major classifications:

1. *Secure/autonomous:* Individuals classified as secure/autonomous describe varied childhood experiences, maintain a balanced view of early relationships, value attachment relationships, and view attachment-related experiences as influential in their development.

2. *Insecure/dismissing:* Adults are classified as insecure on the basis of incoherence, i.e., they have failed to assess and integrate the meaning of those experiential memories. Adults classified as insecure/dismissing deny or devalue the impact of early attachment relationships, have difficulty with recall of specific events, often idealize experiences, and usually describe an early history of rejection.

3. *Insecure/preoccupied:* Adults are classified as insecure on the basis of incoherence, i.e., they have failed to assess and integrate the meaning of those experiential memories. Adults classified as insecure/preoccupied display confusion about past experiences, and current relationships with parents are marked by active anger or passivity.

4. *Unresolved:* Individuals may be classified as unresolved in addition to a major classification. These adults report attachment-related traumas of loss and/or abuse that have not been resolved. The unresolved classification is given precedence over the major classification and is considered an insecure classification.

5. *"Can't Classify":* This category is assigned when scale scores reflect elements rarely seen together in an interview (e.g., high idealization of one parent and high active anger at the other). Such interviews are highly incoherent and insecure.

ADULT ATTACHMENT PATTERNS

Individual or Group

~adapted from Dan Siegel's AAI-inspired questions from *Mindsight,* 2010

SO WHAT?

Why should anyone care about a research instrument? Well, in addition to its utility for the research community, this particular instrument is highly applicable to adults traumatized as children in clinical settings as well. The coded and interpreted interview is predictive of the adult's attachment style to his/her own children. However, in clinical settings it is multipurpose even without its official coding or interpretation.

1. Describe your early family situation: where you were born, where you lived, whether you moved around much, what your caregivers did at various times for a living.

    _____

    _____

    _____

    _____

    _____

2. Describe your relationship with your parents as a young child. Begin as far back as you can remember.

    _____

    _____

    _____

    _____

    _____

3. Please choose five adjectives or words that reflect *your relationship with your mother/caregiver* starting from as far back as you can remember in early childhood—as early as you can go, but say, age 5 to 12 is fine.

    MOTHER (OR PRIMARY CAREGIVER):

    a. _____   b. _____   c. _____

    d. _____   e. _____

4. Think of an example for each word to illustrate a memory or experience that supports the word.

    a. _____

    b. _____

c. _____

d. _____

e. _____

5. Please choose five adjectives or words that reflect *your relationship with your father/caregiver* starting from as far back as you can remember in early childhood—as early as you can go, but say, age 5 to 12 is fine.

   FATHER (OR OTHER CAREGIVER):

   a. _____   b. _____   c. _____

   d. _____   e. _____

6. Think of an example for each word to illustrate a memory or experience that supports the word.

   a. _____

   b. _____

   c. _____

   d. _____

   e. _____

7. Which parent/caregiver did you feel closer to, and why?

   _____

   _____

   _____

   _____

   _____

   _____

8. As a child, when you got upset, what would you do?

   _____

   _____

   _____

   _____

   _____

   _____

   _____

9. What was it like the first time you were separated from your parents or other caregivers?

_____

_____

_____

_____

_____

_____

10. What was it like for you and for them during this separation?

_____

_____

_____

_____

_____

_____

11. If you were sick, injured, or emotionally distressed, what would happen?

_____

_____

_____

_____

_____

12. Were you ever very afraid or terrified of your caregivers? If so, how often?

_____

_____

_____

_____

_____

13. How did your relationship with your caregivers change over time?

_____

_____

_____

_____

_____

14. As a child, did anyone close to you ever die or leave you?

_____

_____

_____

_____

_____

15. How were those losses for you, and how did they impact you and your family?

_____

_____

_____

_____

_____

16. Are you close with your caregivers now?

_____

_____

_____

_____

_____

17. Why do you think they behaved the way that did?

_____

_____

_____

_____

_____

18. What are the main things you've learned about caring for a child from your caregivers?

_____

_____

_____

_____

_____

19. How do you feel all of these issues of your attachment history have affected your ability to be open, to attune, and to resonate with others in your personal or your professional life?

_____

_____

_____

_____

_____

20. Did you find this worksheet difficult? What was most difficult about it?

_____

_____

_____

_____

_____

Family Values

The family of origin is the environment that initially shapes our understanding of what "normal" is for us. Just as attachment isn't necessarily love, "normal" isn't necessarily healthy. As an adult, it's important to examine those values that we introjected as children.

CIRCLE THE FOLLOWING WORDS AND PHRASES THAT ARE MOST DESCRIPTIVE OF THE WAY YOUR FAMILY SYSTEM FUNCTIONED.

FAMILY OF ORIGIN SYSTEM FUNCTION		
Lenient/Permissive	**Open**	**Closed**
Rules are not enforced	Rules are reasonable	Rules are strict
Spoils	Nurtures	Punishes
Unstructured	Structured	Rigidly structured
Unsupervised	Supervision	Rigidly supervised
Disorganized	Flexible	Chaotic or rigid
Ungrounded thinking	OK to think for self	Thinking is done for you
Choices are ignored	Choices	Choices are strictly limited
Lack of direction	Appropriate guidance	Dictatorial
Overly tolerant	Tolerant	Intolerant
Verbal abuse is ignored	Verbally respectful	Verbally abusive
Tirades are ignored	Emotions are allowed	Emotions are punished
Abandoning	Healthy	Abusive
Lost	Freeing	Enslaving

SPIRITUAL VALUES LEARNED AS LITTLE KIDS:

WE LEARNED THAT GOD IS		
Unreliable	Consistent	Strictly rule-bound
Illogical	Balanced	Extreme
Best ignored	Safe	Demanding
Disinterested/unconcerned	Caring	Angry

WRITE OUT YOUR ANSWERS TO THE FOLLOWING QUESTIONS:

Which description(s) above best fits your family of origin experience?

_____

_____

_____

_____

_____

_____

What role(s) best helped you live in your family of origin. *Hero? Overachiever? Rebel? Scapegoat? Lost child? Target child (i.e., singled out for abuse)? Clown? Other?* Give an example:

_____

_____

_____

_____

_____

_____

Describe a typical scene (or two) that illustrates *a day in the life of a child* within your family of origin:

_____

_____

_____

_____

_____

_____

If you are in a family now, choose the category above that best describes your family system:

Lenient/Permissive   Open   Closed

Family Sociograms Group

This is an art project. Well, it's sort of an art project, but unlike most art projects, this one requires *zero talent* in the art department (seriously). You will be plotting your family constellation using a "Sociogram," placing all the focus on the process rather than product.

Developed by Jay Moreno (of psychodrama fame), a sociogram is a graphic representation one's social/ interpersonal relationships. It may be done in groups or individual sessions. The following instructions pertain to groups.

INSTRUCTIONS:

Draw a sociogram of your family.

List the members of your family by placing each name within its own circle on the page. Use a ray (i.e., a solid line with an arrow at the end) to represent any relationships in which one person feels a close attachment to or just plain likes the other. If the feeling is reciprocated, then draw a solid line with arrows at both ends. For any relationships in which the pair is not closely attached or is in conflict with one another, connect them with a broken line.

Once complete, the group breaks up into smaller groups to share their representations with one another. The facilitator might initiate discussion by asking participants to notice the similarities/ differences between each member of their group (e.g., family size, composition, positive and negative relationships, subgroupings).

After some discussion, the larger group comes back together. The facilitator will ask participants to ponder some issues regarding their own family sociograms:

- What circles did you draw first? Why?
- Did you need to change or erase anything? Why?
- Look at the sizes of the circles. How do they compare with one another?
- Where did you place the circles spatially in relation to one another (far away, close to, on top of, below, or next to each other)?
- How complex or simple is the drawing?
- Do you notice any patterns or textures that might be psychologically significant?

Was there anything surprising to you about your sociogram or the exercise in general?

FAMILY, ATTACHMENT AND THE FORMATIVE YEARS

One of the most important needs in childhood is *to be mirrored* by an attuned caretaker. In their landmark book, *Affect Regulation, Mentalization, and the Development of the Self* (2004), Fonagy and colleagues explained that *mirroring* is essential to a child's eventual ability to modulate his/ her own affect states, which is essential to a child's eventual ability regulate him or her *self*. This ability in turn is essential to a child's eventual ability to *mentalize* (i.e., understand another's intention based on his/her behavior), which is essential to a child's eventual ability to be in relationship. Fonagy states, "For Freud in infancy and childhood *others* in the external world are extensions of the self. For us . . . it seems more accurate to see the self as originally an extension of experience of the *other*" (p. 266). It follows that if your *other* was absent, emotionally unavailable, misattuned, or insecurely attached, then those aforementioned abilities may have been compromised.

The poet Maya Angelou wrote, "The ache for home lives in all of us, the safe place where we can go as we are and not be questioned." Unfortunately, for many of us, it is not a longing to return to that place we called home; it is an ache for something that never was. Mercifully, this "ache" need not be a life sentence. Regardless of the circumstances of your childhood, if you are reading this, you found a way to cope and survive it. That's the good news; the bad news is that it is unlikely that you've emerged unscathed—a happy, healthy, securely attached, attuned adult with healthy relational boundaries. Dr. Mary Lou Schack, one of the directors of the Gestalt Therapy Institute of Philadelphia and one of my mentors, has said on many occasions: "Needs that do not get met in childhood become adult needs." It's simple, yet profound, because the implication is that those needs can still be met. We can still become "earned secure" in our adult attachment relationships once those needs get met.

In her book, *Joe Jones*, Anne Lamott put it this way: "After a while the middle-aged person who lives in her head begins to talk to her soul, the kid." Lamott uses *soul*, others use the hackneyed expression "*inner child*"—you know, the one that produces the reflexive eye roll in so many. Love it or hate it, these terms are but symbols for the young, feeling self that was and is. The self that must be revisited in order to provide for him/her the empathic mirroring so sorely missed and so desperately needed.

Although the following exercises may be a bit out of your comfort zone, I encourage you to give each a try. They may save your soul. Or, if that doesn't fit, Martha Beck wrote, "Caring for your inner child has a powerful and surprisingly quick result: Do it and the child heals."

Dialogue with Your Child

A WRITING EXERCISE

INSTRUCTIONS:

You'll need a pen or a pencil, or if you are so inclined you may want to use several colored markers or crayons. On the following pages you will be writing the questions in the left-hand column and the answers in the right-hand column.

1. Using the following page for the writing assignment, begin in the *left-hand column*, using *your dominant hand* (the one with which you write).

2. Begin a conversation with your child part. You might begin with simple introductory questions (e.g. "How are you?" or "How are you feeling?"), whatever questions feel right for you, keeping in mind that the dialogue is with a child.

3. In the *right-hand column*, the child part will be responding to the questions. So, after you have the question written, switch your pen or pencil to *your nondominant hand,* or switch to using a marker or crayon (again hold it with your *nondominant hand*).

4. Read the question and, without forcing anything, wait and see what comes up. Just allow an answer to surface. The answer typically feels as if it is coming from another part of you. Because the dialogue is with the younger part of you, it shouldn't be surprising if the response sounds childlike.

5. When an answer does arise, write it down in the right-hand column.

    It's not uncommon for there to be no response. After all, it's probably been awhile since you've connected to him or her. You may have to ask several times (and maybe on several occasions) before there is enough trust developed between you and the child part that (s)he feels safe enough to be exposed.

6. When the child part does surface, (s)he may write that (s)he is angry with or scared of you. To which you would further inquire as to why that is, and what you can do to help him or her to begin to trust you.

7. Like every other new relationship, its development is a process rather than a one-time exercise. The ultimate goal is to not only access the child part, but to become a nurturing figure to him or her.

ADULT QUESTION (DOMINANT HAND)	CHILD'S RESPONSE (NONDOMINANT HAND)

Developing a Nurturing Voice

ATTACHMENT WORK

> . . .If you ever, ever feel like you're nothing
> you're perfect to me.
> You're so mean
> When you talk about yourself,
> you are wrong
> Change the voices in your head
> Make them like you instead. . .
>
> excerpted from "Perfect" by Pink

Developing a nurturing inner voice is one way to counterbalance the critical parental messages that so many of us have introjected—the voice that keeps telling you that you're not good enough, that something is wrong with you, and what a disappointment you've always been and will always be. Presently, that voice and its messages serve only to limit you and keep you stuck in the past, whereas creating a new one—a responsive, empathic one to calm, soothe and encourage you—would be much more helpful in the present.

EXERCISE 1

Ask yourself these questions:

1. Do I know anybody who has this nurturing quality? (S)he may be real or fictional, it really doesn't matter. Who is it?

2. When you've settled on one person, bring him/her to mind and allow him/her to truly come to life. Picture the person in his/her nurturing aspect. What does this person look like? What is (s)he doing? Perhaps singing to a child, stroking his/her hair? Using a calming voice, when a child is scared? Cooking a favorite meal? Reading a storybook? Whatever feels right.

3. Allow that scene of nurture to become as vivid as possible. Truly listen to the words being said and the tone of voice (s)he is using.

4. Now, imagine being one of the people in the scene, either the child or the nurturing figure, whichever feels right for you. What would it feel like to be that child/nurturing figure? Try taking on that role. Truly embody it for a few minutes.

5. Now imagine a time when you were criticizing yourself. Hear the words you said and the feelings that those words brought up for you.

6. Now consciously switch out of the critical voice and into this more nurturing one—words and tone.

7. Notice what it feels like to be responded to with kindness and compassion instead of criticism.

8. Practice this imaginally a few more times.

9. The next time you find yourself using the critical voice, once again consciously switch out of the critical voice and into this more nurturing one, both words and tone.

10. Practice switching voices as often as you are able.

EXERCISE 2

Remember a time when someone said, "thank you," and you knew that (s)he truly meant it.

1. How did it feel to be acknowledged, appreciated, or loved?

2. Embody that feeling for a few moments.

Now remember a time when a loved one acknowledged something good that you did or said.

1. How did it feel to be acknowledged, appreciated, or loved?

2. Embody that feeling for a few moments.

Now remember a time when you felt appreciated or loved.

1. How did it feel to be acknowledged, appreciated, or loved?

2. Embody that feeling for a few moments.

What do you value most about yourself?

Of the people to whom you matter (and who matter to you), if asked, what would they say they value most in you? What qualities do they admire?

Now, think of your closest friend. If asked, what would (s)he claim to value most in you? Are those things the same (i.e., do you value the same things in you that your friend does)?

What other things about you do you value, but others may not recognize? What are they?

**The following section includes imagery scripts designed exclusively
for furthering this work.**

Multisensory Guided Imagery

According to Belleruth Naparstek, guided imagery is intentional, directed daydreaming, blending one's imagination with words and phrases that evoke sensory fantasy and memory. Guided imagery creates a deeply receptive mind, body, psyche, and spirit state during which change becomes possible. For most of us, imagery is an accessible form of meditation yielding immediate empirically proven benefits, including a wide variety of physical and psychological outcomes. The ones of interest to this population include:

- Reduction of anxiety and depression
- Decrease in blood pressure
- Strengthening of immune function
- Reduction of pain
- Reduction of bingeing and purging in those with bulimia
- Improvement in attention and concentration

Imagery is effective, because it basically bypasses rational thought and logical assumptions, delivering healing messages directly to the hypervigilant primitive brain. Once received, imagery disperses gentle reminders of health, strength, meaning, and hope that affect unconscious assumptions and self-defeating concepts. Because it is processed through the right brain's primitive, sensory, and emotion-based channels, it is an ideal intervention for post-traumatic stress.

Imagery works on the right brain, the home of feeling, sensing, and perceiving, rather than the thinking, judging, analyzing, and deciding functions of the left brain. Because it does not depend on the brain's logical and analytic centers, it circumvents psychological resistance, fear, hopelessness, worry, and doubt, and goes directly to attitude and self-esteem, without interference from the rather obstinate, literal mind that is the domain of the left brain.

Brain development studies have shown that a traumatized brain is impaired in its ability to focus on language or verbal content. Instead, it tends to focus on processing nonverbal danger cues—body movements, facial expressions, and tone of voice—as it searches for information about danger and threat. The primitive brain in effect co-opts cognition and behavior in the service of safety and survival. Unfortunately, this tendency causes some temporary loss in the ability to think abstractly, process language, and attend to ideas or word meanings. These functions are higher cortical functions—gray matter issues—which can only be attended to once the primitive brain is sufficiently calmed. It seems clear that interventions that rely on cognitive, problem-solving activities do not and, more importantly, cannot have much impact on these clients or their terror-driven behavior.

With the advancement of technology, neuroscience has shown us that traumatic changes appear in Broca's area of the brain, where personal experience gets translated into language. It appears that survivors can see, hear, smell, taste, and feel parts of the traumatic event, yet struggle unsuccessfully to translate these sensory elements into language. In addition to this "speechless terror," some long-term trauma survivors experience an additional deficit in their analytical ability. Due to persistently high elevation of stress hormones, which causes a reduction in the size of the hippocampus, survivors are often less able to put things in context and/or make critical distinctions about what is and what is not threatening in the present. Without this necessary discernment, survivors become more and more impulsive and less and less inhibited. In effect, what survivors are left with is a constantly hyperaroused autonomic nervous system, an inability to distinguish past from present threat. This state leads to constant hypervigilance; a speechless terror accompanied by painful and traumatic sensory and body memories and a marked deficiency in their ability to access any of their own cognitive resources. Quite a predicament.

What should be resoundingly apparent to the reader is that <u>talking</u> "about trauma"—which requires participation from the language/ logic portion of the left brain—is inadequate, often retraumatizing to the client. A better option for therapists would be to target the client's highly sensitive, hyperacute right hemisphere with its overfunctioning visual, sensory, and emotional channels. By accessing the limbic system and the right hemisphere of the brain, survivors are able to process the images, body sensations and feelings, attach some sort of meaning to them, and eventually move toward a more helpful and adaptive resolution of the traumatic material.

Recent randomized, controlled studies of military sexual trauma and combat trauma survivors show that imagery offers a viable solution. Using a calming tone of voice, music, and symbolic representations of safety, imagery quiets the hypervigilant primitive brain, creating an environment where the higher brain can once again function in the service of the survivor.

Naparstek posits that guided imagery provides a cushion of evocative, multisensory protective images and built-in emotional safety. Appealing memories and lush fantasies require little energy or discipline to evoke. They provide distraction from pain and carry clients beyond worry, fear, and anguish. She goes on to report that guided imagery has the ability to avoid the direct traps of language and literalism. It is a powerful healing tool that provides a kinder, gentler and more effective route to tending to wounds of the inner self. Naparstek explains that the imaginary world developed through imagery is a generous place where clients can gain distance by locking pain away in a safe, floating it away on the wind, or erasing it from an imaginary blackboard. In this world, clients can summon protection and support from magical allies, remembered friends, favorite animals, powerful ancestors, guardian angels, and other divine helpers. They can create as many layers of distance between the traumatic event and themselves as needed, all the while surrounding themselves with loving, powerful protectors.

For more information regarding multisensory guided imagery, the reader is referred to Belleruth Naparstek's website: *www.healthjourneys.com.*

Further Reading: B. Naparstek, *Invisible Heroes: Survivors of Trauma and How They Heal* (New York: Bantam, 2004).

Clinicians (and others) are invited to make their own audio recordings (for clients to download) of the following multisensory guided imagery scripts. Visit the ***Audio Recordings Page*** of the Trauma 101 website at **www.trauma101.com.**

The purpose of your recording of the scripts for your clients is twofold:

1. The explicit message contained within the script, along with the *transition object** that the familiar human voice provides.

2. Once recorded, the clinician's reading of the script is combined with a musical background that when listened to (with headphones or earbuds) provides the listener with an auditory form of alternating bilateral stimulation.

FYI: *The use of alternating right, left stimulation (i.e., both hemispheres) is for the purpose of activating both hemispheres for processing and integrating information.*

---

* Many clients find it helpful to have concrete transitional objects as well. One way for clinicians to present such objects to clients is to offer him/her an array of stones, feathers, pieces of driftwood, etc., and invite him or her to choose the one that is most attractive. Allow the client to hold and handle the object during session, then ask the client if (s)he would like to take it with him/her. Subsequently, the object can serve as a mediator and "transitional object" in the literal sense of the term, namely as a "third object" between the client and the clinician. Its purpose is to evoke memories of the interactions between client and clinician and the positive emotions associated with the attachment relationship.

Containment Imagery Script

"The Container" is an imaginal resource that addresses the need to compartmentalize the distressing material, in order to be present in the here and now, attending to what one needs to. Be clear: This script is not a repression or suppression of memories, thoughts, affect, or emotion. It is a technique employed to allow one to attend to what (s)he needs to attend to until (s)he has the necessary resources to attend to those distressing/disturbing memories, thoughts, affects, or emotions. (**Remember: Time is a resource.**)

CLINICIAN READS:

Allow yourself to be comfortable . . . either lying down or sitting up with your back, neck, and spine fully supported. Knowing that you will not be interrupted for the next little while, begin by gently closing your eyes.

(Clinician should breathe audibly with the exhalation longer than the inhalation.)

Now begin to bring your attention to your breath—the direct experience of your breath—however it is . . . and however it changes. Allow yourself to softly focus your awareness on to the breath that is arising right now—the in-breath and the out-breath, the rising and the falling. If you can, try to follow one full cycle of the breath from the beginning of the in-breath through its entirety and then to the beginning of the out-breath through its entirety. Allow yourself the time and the space to be in direct contact with the breath throughout one entire cycle.

(Clinician should breathe audibly with the exhalation longer than the inhalation.)

As you continue to pay attention to the breath, you may notice distractions that arise. Just allow yourself to notice those distractions . . . any bodily sensations or any thoughts that may arise. If possible, allow yourself to become aware of the separateness of those bodily sensations—notice how those sensations are separate and distinct from your thoughts, your ideas, and your words.

(Clinician should breathe audibly with the exhalation longer than the inhalation.)

Now, as you continue with this focused awareness, you will notice how often you lose contact with the breath . . . maybe you become caught in a thought or an idea or plan, or maybe some other bodily sensation pulls your attention. When a distraction happens, simply notice that you have lost connection with the breath, and gently bring your awareness back.

(Clinician should breathe with the exhalation longer than the inhalation.)

We'll begin now with a deep breath in through your nose . . . inhaling slowly and deeply. Exhale through pursed lips until all the air has been released.

(Clinician should breathe audibly with the exhalation longer than the inhalation.)

Now we are going to be creating a container. It doesn't matter what kind of container it is, as long as it can "hold" any and all disturbing material. If you were going to develop such a container, what would it look like? Some people have used boxes, safes, trunks, or chests; others have used bookbags, knapsacks, or other pieces of luggage. It can be anything really, a tank, a submarine, an underground well—anything that suits you.

(Clinician should breathe audibly with the exhalation longer than the inhalation.)

Can you bring to mind an image of something like that—something that would be able to contain any and all disturbing material? When you have one in mind, take a good look at it. What material is it made out of? How is it held together? How big is it? What color is it? Are there any markings on it? If there are markings, notice them; if not, that's fine. But I'd like you to add something to this container. I'd like you to add in some way—whether it be a note or a sign or an inscription of sort—a notation to indicate that this container will remain tightly sealed. It will remain tightly sealed until you wish to open it and retrieve something from it. Otherwise it will remain sealed. It can be opened—but only by you—and it should be opened only in the service of your healing.

(Clinician should breathe audibly with the exhalation longer than the inhalation.)

So once again, look at your container. Does it already have that message on it? If not, place it on there now.

(Pause.)

Now, how does this container open? Are you able to open it by yourself, or do you need help? Is there a lock on it? If not, feel free to put one or several on it now.

(Pause.)

(Clinician should breathe audibly with the exhalation longer than the inhalation.)

Once the locks are in place, we'll experiment with opening and closing them, locking and unlocking them. As you do that, notice how much, or how little, effort it takes to open and close the container.

(Clinician should breathe audibly with the exhalation longer than the inhalation.)

When you feel comfortable handling it, I'd like you to think of something that you might put into the container—just for practice. Do whatever is necessary to open it up, and then place something in there. When I say "something," I mean anything, really, that may be distressing or disturbing to you right now. It could be thoughts or worries, bad feelings or bad memories . . . it could be something that you have to do but not right this minute. Or it could be something that keeps you from being present with this exercise. It could be self-judgment, doubt, or pain. Whatever it is, you're going to put it into the container . . . whatever you need to do to get it in there, do that now.

(Pause.)

(Clinician should breathe audibly with the exhalation longer than the inhalation.)

Once the disturbing material is in, close it up and lock the container. (Pause.) Now, breathe deeply as you look at the locked container, securely holding anything that you need or want it to hold.

(Breathe audibly with the exhalation longer than the inhalation.)

Notice how you feel in your body having set aside whatever distressing thing you put in your container. Can you sense that it is fully contained? Is there something that keeps it from feeling fully contained? If so, can we try opening your container and putting that in there as well? Remember that this container is yours and will hold anything and everything you need it to hold for as long as you need it to.

(Clinician should breathe audibly with the exhalation longer than the inhalation.)

Now imagine walking away from your container so that it is no longer in your sight. Notice the feeling in your body now that you are no longer burdened by what you put in the container. Notice your breath—your in-breath and your out-breath—and any sensations of relief you feel in your body. Maybe your shoulders have dropped a bit, or some of the tension in your neck has subsided. Whatever feelings of relief you notice, breathe deeply and just notice.

Whatever you put in the container is now securely locked inside. It is for you to open whenever you wish to put things in or take them out.

So now, just for practice, let's go back to your container. Once you have it in sight, look closely. See if you can read what is written on the outside. (Pause.) Continue focusing on your breath as you continue to approach the container. When you are within reach, unlock it and open it up. As you open it notice that what you put in there is still there, separate from you. You might want to put something else in, or maybe even a few things. Or you may just wish to lock it back up. Whatever feels right and safe to you, do that now.

(Pause.)

(Clinician should breathe audibly with the exhalation longer than the inhalation.)

And once you're finished practicing putting things in your container and securely locking it back up, you can walk away from the container. As you walk away, begin to bring yourself and your awareness back to this room. Know that this resource—this secure container—is available to you at any time. Know that you can use it to hold any and all disturbing things. Know that all the things that you have chosen—or anything that you choose to contain in the future—will be secure and will remain secure. You can access the material whenever you feel ready to do so. But for now, you may leave it, knowing it is safely and securely contained.

(Clinician should breathe audibly with the exhalation longer than the inhalation.)

And now, whenever you are ready, gently bring yourself back to the room by counting up from one to five. When you reach the number five, your eyes will gently open. You will be awake and alert, and feeling only peace. One . . . two . . . three. Take a deep breath . . . four . . . and five.

Comfortable Place Script

Imagery designed to facilitate the development and introjection of a comfortable (safe or neutral) place. The objective here, as with many of the guided imagery meditations, is to decrease sympathetic activation (i.e., quiet the fight/flight response) by activating the parasympathetic nervous system. Subsequent listening provides reinforcement and the *relishing* of this positive experience.

Allow yourself to be comfortable . . . either lying down or sitting up with your back, neck, and spine fully supported. Knowing that you will not be interrupted for the next little while, begin by gently closing your eyes.

(Clinician should breathe audibly with the exhalation longer than the inhalation.)

Now begin to bring your attention to the direct experience of your breath, however it is . . . and however it changes. Allow yourself to softly focus your awareness on the breath that is arising right now . . . the in-breath and the out-breath . . . the rising and the falling. If you can, try to follow one full cycle of the breath from the beginning of the in-breath through its entirety to the beginning of the out-breath through its entirety. Allow yourself the time and the space to be in direct contact with the breath throughout one entire cycle.

(Clinician should breathe audibly with the exhalation longer than the inhalation.)

As you continue to pay attention to the breath, you may notice distractions that arise. Just allow yourself to notice those distractions, any bodily sensations and any thoughts that may arise. If possible, allow yourself to become aware of the separateness of those bodily sensations. Notice how those sensations are separate and distinct from your thoughts, your ideas, and your words.

(Clinician should breathe audibly with the exhalation longer than the inhalation.)

Now, as you continue with this focused awareness, you will notice how often you lose contact with the breath . . . maybe you become caught in a thought or an idea or plan or maybe some other bodily sensation has pulled your attention. When a distraction happens, simply notice that you have lost connection with the breath, and gently bring your awareness back to the breath.

(Clinician should breathe audibly with the exhalation longer than the inhalation.)

We'll begin now with a deep breath in through your nose, inhaling slowly and deeply. Exhale through pursed lips until all the air has been released.

(Clinician should breathe audibly with the exhalation longer than the inhalation.)

We are going to be creating a silent, healing space all around you. In order to do that, focus only on your breath and the sound of my voice. As you begin to let go, I'm going to count from eight to one. And with each descending number, find yourself becoming more and more relaxed, more and more able to stay connected to your breath, and more and more able to stay with the sound of my voice as you continue letting go. Eight . . . allow your breath to relax your body, gently inhaling. Seven . . . bring the breath deep down, lowering all the way. Six . . . allow the relaxation to gently drift throughout your body as you go deeper still. Five . . . let go, as the breath deepens and you feel those muscles softening. Four . . . as the relaxation gently encloses your heart and your lungs, you're aware of deep comfort, deep relaxation. Notice how gentle and quiet your breathing is becoming. Three . . . notice as each breath allows you to become more and more relaxed, and going deeper, you relax. Two . . . more and more relaxed and letting go. And one . . . you now find yourself outdoors in a very, very comfortable place. Perhaps it is a place that is new to you. Or maybe you have been here many times in real life or in the beauty of your own mind. You see this beautifully serene place. Allow the images to come. For in this place of beauty and comfort—your place of comfort—you may invite anyone you like, or you may prefer to keep this place private. Either is fine, as long you remain perfectly comfortable.

(Clinician should breathe audibly with the exhalation longer than the inhalation.)

In this place of serenity, you know only peace. Allow the images to come. Notice the color of the sky at your favorite time of day. And in this place, at this most perfect time of day, at the season and the temperature that you like on your skin, allow your senses to become more and more awake. Drink in the surroundings you allow yourself to see; if not with your eyes, then sense with your heart. . . . Each time you come here, you will develop it and allow it to become more and more beautiful. Allow yourself to see what is here now. . . . Notice the colors around you. Let the colors and textures come alive as you look from side to side, up and down. See what makes this place so perfect for you. Now listen . . . what do you hear in this place, what do you hear that lets you know that this your ideal place? And breathing in the beauty and the comfort of this place, you may notice certain scents . . . the smell of the air, or the sweet smell of a nature all around you. Breathe in the smells of your ideal place. . . . Let yourself bask in the comfort and beauty and the peace. Allow yourself to walk around, to be in this place, to notice more and more of what is here for you in this place. . . . Here is a place where you may create anything you like.

(Pause 15 seconds.)

(Clinician should breathe audibly with the exhalation longer than the inhalation.)

If you feel like it, you may build special places for special kinds of feelings that need to be healed, special places to wash away fear and pain . . . perhaps a waterfall or a healing pool of water. You may wish to stand under the waterfall: wash away whatever should be washed away . . . anything that you'd like to be finished with. Each time you come to the waterfall or the healing pool of water, you can wash away more and more of the past . . . more and more of what no longer fits . . . more and more of what no longer serves you. . . . You may plan to use these waters again the next time you visit.

(Pause 15 seconds.)

(Clinician should breathe audibly with the exhalation longer than the inhalation.)

For now, allow yourself to begin walking around this . . . your . . . place. As you do, you come upon your very favorite spot . . . the best of all places.

[Long pause.] As you arrive, feel free to sit down and get comfortable. Breathe in the serenity . . . the peace.

(Clinician should breathe audibly with the exhalation longer than the inhalation.)

As you take a final look around, you breathe in . . . knowing absolutely that this is your place . . . that you have been here before . . . you are welcome here. You belong . . . and you may return any time you like.

(Clinician should breathe audibly with the exhalation longer than the inhalation.)

And when you are ready, gently bring yourself back to the room by counting up
from one to five. When you reach the number five, your eyes will gently open.
You will be awake and alert, and feeling only peace. One . . . two . . . three. Take a
deep breath . . . four . . . and five.

*Repair*enting:
Imagery for Disrupted Attachment

This imagery exercise is designed to facilitate the development and introjection of an emotionally attuned, mirroring, nurturing attachment figure—a competent inner parent providing unconditional positive regard—not unlike Winnicott's "good-enough mother."

Allow yourself to be comfortable, either lying down or sitting up, with your back, neck, and spine fully supported. Knowing that you will not be interrupted for the next little while, begin by gently closing your eyes.

(Clinician should breathe audibly with the exhalation longer than the inhalation.)

Now bring your attention to the direct experience of your breath—however it is, and however it changes. Allow yourself to softly focus your awareness on the breath that is arising right now . . . the in-breath and the out-breath . . . the rising and the falling. If you can, try to follow one full cycle of the breath from the beginning of the in-breath through its entirety to the beginning of the out-breath through its entirety. Allow yourself the time and the space to be in direct contact with the breath throughout one entire cycle.

(Clinician should breathe audibly with the exhalation longer than the inhalation.)

As you continue to pay attention to the breath, you may notice distractions that arise. Just allow yourself to notice those distractions . . . any bodily sensations and any thoughts that may arise. If possible, allow yourself to become aware of the separateness of those bodily sensations. Notice how those sensations are separate—distinct from your thoughts, your ideas, and your words.

(Clinician should breathe audibly with the exhalation longer than the inhalation.)

Now, as you continue with this focused awareness, you will notice how often you lose contact with the breath . . . maybe you become caught in a thought or an idea or plan or maybe some other bodily sensation pulls your attention. When a distraction happens, simply notice that you have lost connection with the breath, and gently bring your awareness back to the breath.

(Clinician should breathe audibly with the exhalation longer than the inhalation.)

Gently bring your awareness to any sensations in your body. Notice any tension, pressure, tightness, warmth, coolness, pain, or other recognizable sensations. You may also notice that the thinking part of your brain wants to label these sensations. Allow it, and then gently return your awareness to the direct experience of the sensations themselves. If you'd like, begin to notice sensations in various parts of the body. You might begin with the feet, working your way up the body . . . noticing the ankles, shins, knees, thighs, buttocks, hips, lower back, upper back, shoulders, biceps, elbows, forearms, wrists, hands . . . now beginning again at the neck . . . jaw . . . behind and under the eyes, forehead, crown of the head, and finally the back of the head. If you'd like, you may consciously relax any overly tight muscles—noticing your choice to do so or not.

Maintain this awareness for the next little while.

(Wait 45 seconds.)

Now gently allow your attention and awareness to rest on any sensations in the abdomen or belly area. Notice any sensations—whether "comfort" or "discomfort." Without any effort to distract yourself from them or to change them, allow the sensations to just be there. If you do try to get rid of them or distract yourself from them, simply notice that you have done so, then gently return your awareness to the sensations.

Maintain this awareness for the next little while.

(Wait 45 seconds.)

Now, with a gentle breath, bring to mind a time when you were close to—that is, physically close to—somebody; somebody you could trust, fully and completely. It could be anybody: a parent or grandparent, sister or brother, or a family member; it could be a friend, a partner, or anybody else—anyone with whom you have had many experiences of complete trust.

If you are unable to conjure such a person, bring to mind a childhood pet to whom you felt connected and whom you trusted completely.

Bring to mind the image of this person or pet. Invite this person or animal to be here with you now. Take as much time as you need to feel this presence fully. Look deeply into the face of this person or pet, seeing as clearly as you can. While gazing into one another's eyes, take a few deep breaths—holding this experience of connection.

Now bring to mind a time in your early childhood when you felt happy—just comfortable, unworried, and at ease . . . it may be a time when you were with this trusted person or pet. With that image in your mind, gently bring your attention to your abdomen, noticing any sensations associated with this memory of contentment and happiness in childhood.

Looking deeply into the face of the person or pet, notice their reaction to your experience of this fond memory. Perhaps you see no reaction, and if that is the case, simply notice and then return to your attention to your own emotions and bodily sensations. If you see a reaction on the face of the person or pet, notice it . . . and then again notice your own emotions and bodily sensations and/or feelings about the other's reaction.

Maintain this awareness for the next little while.

(Wait 45 seconds.)

Now, bring to mind a time in your early childhood when you felt emotional discomfort—maybe a time when you felt threatened, frightened, frustrated, angry, helpless, or ashamed and humiliated.

Begin looking deeply into the face of the person or pet and notice their reaction to your experience of this unpleasant memory. Perhaps you see no reaction, and if that is the case, simply notice and then return your attention to your own emotions and bodily sensations. If you see a reaction on the face of the person or pet, notice it . . . and then again, notice your own emotions and bodily sensations and/or feelings about their reaction.

Try and stay with this experience of your mutual reactions for at least 15 seconds.

Now, letting go of that image, refocus your attention on your breath—the direct experience of the breath—however it is . . . and however it changes. Allow yourself to softly focus your awareness on the breath that is arising right now . . . the in-breath and the out-breath . . . the rising and the falling. If you can, try to follow one full cycle of the breath from the beginning of the in-breath through its entirety to the beginning of the out-breath through its entirety. Allow yourself the time and the space to be in direct contact with the breath throughout one entire cycle.

(Clinician should breathe audibly with the exhalation longer than the inhalation.)

Now, consider the possibility that you may presently have such a person or pet within your own mind. Allow yourself to conjure an image or concept of such a being . . . allow it to take any shape or form.

Give yourself a few moments to observe this being. Notice its qualities. . . . Does it appear soothing? Receptive and attuned? Kind? Concerned? Understanding? Does it appear forgiving? Charitable? Patient and tolerant? Does it seem as capable and competent? Reliable and trustworthy? Nurturing and devoted as the person or pet with whom you interacted just a few minutes ago?

Now, make some gentle inquiries about this being, "Does this being appear to be disapproving and judgmental or loving and accepting? Does it appear to be kind and generous or mean-spirited and inconsiderate? Does this being appear to provide safety and security or does it appear dangerous? How do you feel about this entity? Do you trust this entity or not?"

With this new entity in mind, gently allow yourself to notice any sensations in your body . . . paying particular attention to your abdomen . . . noticing any feelings that come up around this being. Just for a moment, withholding any labels or judgments, allow the sensations and feelings to remain in your awareness.

(Wait 45 seconds.)

Now, keeping this being close, bring to mind a time in your early childhood when you felt happy—just comfortable, unworried, and at ease. With this image in your mind, gently bring your attention once again to your abdomen—noticing any sensations associated with this memory of contentment and happiness in childhood.

Now, looking deeply into the face of this being, notice the other's reaction to your experience of this fond memory. Perhaps you see no reaction, and if that is the case, simply notice and then return to your attention to your own emotions and bodily sensations. If you see a reaction on the face of this being, just notice it . . . and then once again, notice your own emotions and bodily sensations and/or feelings about the other's reaction.

(Wait 45 seconds.)

Again, keeping this being close, bring to mind a time in your early childhood when you felt emotionally uncomfortable—maybe a time when you felt threatened, frightened, frustrated, angry, helpless, or ashamed and humiliated.

Looking deeply into the face of this being, notice the other's reaction to your experience of this memory. Perhaps you see no reaction, and if that is the case, simply notice and then return to your attention to your own emotions and bodily sensations. If you see a reaction on the face of the being, notice it . . . and then again, notice your own emotions and bodily sensations and/ or feelings about the other's reaction.

Now, with a gentle breath, begin to notice any appraisals, assessments, judgments, opinions, beliefs, interpretations, or any other ideas that occur as you continue to focus on your bodily sensations, feelings, and/or emotions as they relate to what you have experienced during this meditation.

(Wait 20 seconds.)

Now, letting go of that image, refocus your attention on your breath—the direct experience of the breath—however it is . . . and however it changes. Allow yourself to softly focus your awareness onto the breath that is arising right now . . . the in-breath and the out-breath . . . the rising and the falling. If you can, try to follow one full cycle of the breath from the beginning of the in-breath through its entirety to the beginning of the out-breath through its entirety. Allow yourself the time and the space to be in direct contact with the breath throughout one entire cycle.

(Clinician should breathe audibly with the exhalation longer than the inhalation.)

And when you are ready, begin to notice the chair or bed beneath you. Pay attention to the sensations in your feet. Now your hands . . . gently make a fist, then release it, stretching your fingers wide. Now, bring yourself back to this room by slowly counting up from one to five. When you reach the number five, your eyes will gently open. You will be awake and alert, and feeling only peace. One . . . two . . . three. Take a deep breath . . . four . . . and five.

Imagery for Care and Nurture Script

This imagery is designed to facilitate the development and introjection of a direct experience of care and nurture.

Allow yourself to be comfortable—either lying down or sitting up with your back, neck, and spine fully supported. Knowing that you will not be interrupted for the next little while, begin by gently closing your eyes.

(Clinician should breathe audibly with the exhalation longer than the inhalation.)

Now, begin to bring your attention to your breath—the direct experience of your breath—however it is . . . and however it changes. Allow yourself to softly focus your awareness on the breath that is arising right now . . . the in-breath and the out-breath . . . the rising and the falling. If you can, try to follow one full cycle of the breath from the beginning of the in-breath through its entirety to the beginning of the out-breath through its entirety. Allow yourself the time and the space to be in direct contact with the breath throughout one entire cycle.

(Clinician should breathe audibly with the exhalation longer than the inhalation.)

As you continue to pay attention to the breath, you may notice distractions that arise. Just allow yourself to notice those distractions . . . any bodily sensations or any thoughts that may arise. If possible, allow yourself to become aware of the separateness of those bodily sensations, Notice how those sensations are separate, distinct from your thoughts, your ideas, and your words.

(Clinician should breathe audibly with the exhalation longer than the inhalation.)

Now, as you continue with this focused awareness, you may notice how often you lose contact with the breath . . . maybe you become caught in a thought or an idea or plan or maybe some other bodily sensation has pulled your attention. When a distraction happens, simply notice that you have lost connection with the breath, and gently bring your awareness back to the breath.

(Clinician should breathe audibly with the exhalation longer than the inhalation.)

We'll begin now with a deep breath in through your nose . . . inhaling slowly and deeply. Exhale through pursed lips until all the air has been released.

(Clinician should breathe audibly with the exhalation longer than the inhalation.)

Now, I would like you to bring to mind a time when you felt cared for . . . a time when someone tended to your needs . . . someone took care of you . . . made sure that you were all right. If a particular incident or person doesn't immediately come to mind, allow yourself to imagine such an incident. Allow the incident—real or imagined—to take shape. Bring into focus the image of the person who is caring for you.

(Pause.)

What does this person look like? Now, look into this person's eyes . . . what do you see? What features stand out? What features make you feel cared for and bring comfort to you? Perhaps a smile . . . or a soft voice . . . a gentle touch . . . whatever it is that brings you comfort from this person . . . allow that to happen now.

(Pause.)

(Clinician should breathe audibly with the exhalation longer than the inhalation.)

As you continue to allow this person to care for you in a way that brings you comfort, begin to notice any emotions that you may feel . . . just notice your response to the gentle care this person continues to offer.

(Pause.)

(Clinician should breathe audibly with the exhalation longer than the inhalation.)

Allow the feelings of comfort to spread, noticing all of the sensations in your body . . . as this person who cares for you very deeply . . . stays with you . . . comforting and supporting you in a way that is perfect for you.

(Pause.)

(Clinician should breathe audibly with the exhalation longer than the inhalation.)

This person will stay with you for as long as you would like. Continue to breathe in the support all around you. And know that, at any time, you can return to this caring person whenever you feel like it.

(Clinician should breathe audibly with the exhalation longer than the inhalation.)

And when you are ready, gently bring yourself back to the room by counting up from one to five. When you reach the number five, your eyes will gently open. You will be awake and alert, and feeling only peace. One . . . two . . . three. Take a deep breath . . . four . . . and five.

Imagery for Addiction: Longings/Cravings

This imagery is designed to promote distress tolerance, self-empowerment, and self-efficacy.

Allow yourself to be comfortable . . . either lying down or sitting up with your back, neck, and spine fully supported. Knowing that you will not be interrupted for the next little while, begin by gently closing your eyes.

(Clinician should breathe audibly with the exhalation longer than the inhalation.)

Now begin to bring your attention to your breath—the direct experience of your breath—however it is . . . and however it changes. Allow yourself to softly focus your awareness on the breath that is arising right now . . . the in-breath and the out-breath . . . the rising and the falling. If you can, try to follow one full cycle of the breath from the beginning of the in-breath through its entirety to the beginning of the out-breath through its entirety. Allow yourself the time and space to be in direct contact with the breath throughout one entire cycle.

(Clinician should breathe audibly with the exhalation longer than the inhalation.)

As you continue to pay attention to the breath, you may notice distractions that arise. Just allow yourself to notice those distractions . . . any bodily sensations and any thoughts that may arise. If possible, allow yourself to become aware of the separateness of those bodily sensations. Notice how those sensations are separate, distinct from your thoughts, your ideas, and your words.

(Clinician should breathe audibly with the exhalation longer than the inhalation.)

Now, as you continue with this focused awareness, you will notice how often you lose contact with the breath . . . maybe you become caught in a thought or an idea or plan or maybe some other bodily sensation pulls your attention. When a distraction happens, simply notice that you have lost connection with the breath, and gently bring your awareness back to the breath.

(Clinician should breathe audibly with the exhalation longer than the inhalation.)

We'll begin now with a deep breath in through your nose . . . inhaling slowly and deeply. Exhale through pursed lips until all the air has been released.

(Clinician should breathe audibly with the exhalation longer than the inhalation.)

Gently bring your awareness to any sensations in your body. Notice any tension, pressure, tightness, warmth, coolness, pain, or other recognizable sensations. You may also notice that the thinking part of your brain wants to label these sensations. Allow it, and then gently return your awareness to the direct experience of the sensations themselves. If you'd like, begin to notice sensations in various parts of the body. You might begin with the feet, working your way up the body . . . noticing the ankles, shins, knees, thighs, buttocks, hips, lower back, upper back, shoulders, biceps, elbows, forearms, wrists, hands . . . now beginning again at the neck . . .

jaw . . . behind and under the eyes, forehead, crown of the head, and finally the back of the head. If you'd like, you may consciously relax any overly tight muscles—noticing your choice to do so or not.

Maintain this awareness for the next little while.

(Wait 45 seconds.)

Now, gently allow your attention and awareness to rest on any sensations in the abdomen or belly area. Notice any sensations, whether "comfortable" or "uncomfortable." Without any effort to distract yourself from them or to change them, allow the sensations to just be there. If you do try to get rid of them or distract yourself from them, simply notice that you have done so, and then gently return your awareness the sensations. Maintain this awareness for the next little while.

(Wait 45 seconds.)

Now, with a gentle breath, bring to mind a time when you felt mildly upset about not getting something that you wanted, maybe something that you felt you deserved. Bring to mind an image of that object of your desire or craving. Study it. What does it look like? Sound like? Feel like? If it has an odor or fragrance, inhale its scent. Give yourself some time to be with this object of your desire.

(Wait 45 seconds.)

With the object in mind, gently allow yourself to notice any emotions . . . any sensations in your body . . . any feelings that come up around the desired object. Just for a moment, withholding any labels or judgments, allow the sensations and feelings to remain in awareness. If they happen to slip from awareness, and you begin analyzing, labeling or judging, just notice and gently bring yourself back to the feelings, sensations, or emotions. Maintain this awareness for the next little while.

(Wait 45 seconds.)

Now, with a gentle breath, begin to notice any appraisals, assessments, judgments, opinions, beliefs, interpretations, or any other ideas that occur as you continue to focus on your bodily sensations, feelings, and/or emotions as they relate to what you have experienced during this meditation.

(Wait 20 seconds.)

Now, refocus your attention on your breath—the direct experience of the breath—however it is . . . and however it changes. Allow yourself to softly focus your awareness on the breath that is arising right now . . . the in-breath and the out-breath . . . the rising and the falling. If you can, try to follow one full cycle of the breath from the beginning of the in-breath through its entirety to the beginning of the out-breath through its entirety. Allow yourself the time and space to be in direct contact with the breath throughout one entire cycle.

(Clinician should breathe audibly with the exhalation longer than the inhalation.)

Now, with a gentle breath, bring to mind a time when you felt pretty upset—but not overwhelmed—about not getting something that you really wanted . . . maybe something that you felt you deserved. Bring to mind an image of that object of your desire or craving. Study it. What does it look like? Sound like? Feel like? If it has an odor or fragrance, inhale its scent. Give yourself some time to be with this object of your desire.

(Wait 45 seconds.)

With the object in mind, gently allow yourself to notice any emotions . . . any sensations in your body . . . any feelings that come up around the desired object. Just for the moment, withholding any labels or judgments, just allow the sensations and feelings to remain in awareness. If they happen to slip from awareness, and you begin analyzing, labeling or judging, just notice and gently bring yourself back to the feelings, sensations, or emotions.

Maintain this awareness for the next little while.

(Wait 45 seconds.)

Now, with a gentle breath, begin to notice any appraisals, assessments, judgments, opinions, beliefs, interpretations, or any other ideas that occur as you continue to focus on your bodily sensations, feelings, and/or emotions as they relate to what you have experienced during this meditation.

(Wait 20 seconds.)

Now refocus your attention on your breath—the direct experience of the breath—however it is . . . and however it changes. Allow yourself to softly focus your awareness on the breath that is arising right now . . . the in-breath and the out-breath . . .the rising and the falling. If you can, try to follow one full cycle of the breath from the beginning of the in-breath through its entirety to the beginning of the out-breath through its entirety. Allow yourself the time and space to be in direct contact with the breath throughout one entire cycle.

(Clinician should breathe audibly with the exhalation longer than the inhalation.)

Now, with a gentle breath, bring to mind a time when you felt pretty upset—but not overwhelmed—about not getting something that you really wanted, maybe something that you felt you deserved. Bring to mind an image of that object of your desire or craving. Study it. What does it look like? Sound like? Feel like? If it has an odor or fragrance, inhale its scent. Give yourself some time to be with this object of your desire.

(Wait 45 seconds.)

With the object in mind, gently allow yourself to notice any emotions . . . any sensations in your body . . . any feelings that come up around the desired object. Just for the moment, withholding any labels or judgments, just allow the sensations and feelings to remain in awareness. If they happen to slip from awareness, and you begin analyzing, labeling or judging, just notice and gently bring yourself back to the feelings, sensations, or emotions.

Maintain this awareness for the next little while.

(Wait 45 seconds.)

Now, with a gentle breath, begin to notice any appraisals, assessments, judgments, opinions, beliefs, interpretations, or any other ideas that occur as you continue to focus on your bodily sensations, feelings, and/or emotions as they relate to what you have experienced during this meditation.

(Wait 45 seconds.)

Now refocus your attention on your breath—the direct experience of the breath—however it is . . . and however it changes. Allow yourself to softly focus your awareness on the breath that is arising right now . . . the in-breath and the out-breath . . . the rising and the falling. If you can, try to follow one full cycle of the breath from the beginning of the in-breath through its entirety to the beginning of the out-breath through its entirety. Allow yourself the time and the space to be in direct contact with the breath throughout one entire cycle.

(Clinician should breathe audibly with the exhalation longer than the inhalation.)

Now, with a gentle breath, bring to mind a time when you felt very upset about not getting something that you wanted. Bring to mind an image of that object of your desire or craving. Study it. What does it look like? Sound like? Feel like? If it has an odor or fragrance, inhale its scent. Give yourself some time to be with this object of your desire.

(Wait 45 seconds.)

With the object in mind, gently allow yourself to notice any emotions . . . any sensations in your body . . . any feelings that come up around the desired object. Just for a moment, withholding any labels or judgments, allow the sensations and feelings to remain in awareness. If they happen to slip from awareness, and you begin analyzing, labeling or judging, just notice and gently bring yourself back to the feelings, sensations, or emotions.

Maintain this awareness for the next little while.

(Wait 45 seconds.)

Now, with a gentle breath, begin to notice any appraisals, assessments, judgments, opinions, beliefs, interpretations, or any other ideas that occur as you continue to focus on your bodily sensations, feelings, and/or emotions as they relate to what you have experienced during this meditation.

(Wait 20 seconds.)

Now refocus your attention on your breath—the direct experience of the breath—however it is . . . and however it changes. Allow yourself to softly focus your awareness on the breath that is arising right now . . . the in-breath and the out-breath . . . the rising and the falling. If you can, try to follow one full cycle of the breath from the beginning of the in-breath through its entirety to the beginning of the out-breath through its entirety. Allow yourself the time and the space to be in direct contact with the breath throughout one entire cycle.

(Clinician should breathe audibly with the exhalation longer than the inhalation.)

And when you are ready, begin to notice the chair or bed beneath you. Pay attention to the sensations in your feet. Now your hands . . . gently make a fist, then release it, stretching your fingers wide. Now bring yourself back to this room by slowly counting up from one to five. When you reach the number five, your eyes will gently open. You will be awake and alert, and feeling only peace. One . . . two . . . three. Take a deep breath . . . four . . . and five.

Boundaries

Bound·a·ry noun (pl. *boundaries*): A line that marks the limits of an area; a dividing line: a boundary wall. Often **boundaries**: a limit of a subject or sphere of activity

Inherent in all relationships are underlying assumptions that are based on current societal norms and values. These assumptions dictate one's repertoire of acceptable behaviors given the nature of the particular relationship and his/her role within that relationship. If everyone were aware of, and in full agreement with, these assumptions, perhaps the need to set and maintain personal boundaries would not be quite so important. But, given the givens. . . .

PERSONAL BOUNDARIES WITHIN RELATIONSHIPS

Boundaries are the internal and external lines that we draw to protect ourselves and others. They help to define who we are, who we're not, and with whom we're willing to share that information. Boundaries appear at a variety of places in an individual's psyche and body: sensory tolerances, preferences regarding physical proximity, levels of stimulation, degree of activity, etc. Boundaries monitor and regulate the degree of personal space within relationships. Healthy boundaries are situationally flexible. Boundaries that are too rigid prevent growth and exchange with sources of energy outside the boundary, while boundaries that are too porous fail to protect the person within the boundary. So we are constantly setting, shifting, negotiating, and renegotiating our personal boundaries with regards to people, proximity, and personal information.

The five categories of boundaries include:

- **Physical:** Who, when, how, and how much others may touch me, and vice versa.
- **Emotional:** What do I consider acceptable treatment within the relationship? Do others respect and treat me well? Do I reciprocate?
- **Spiritual:** How much of my belief system, spirituality, and practices do I feel comfortable sharing? When and with whom?
- **Sexual:** When, with whom, and how much of my sexuality and beliefs about sexuality do I share? Note that sexual boundaries go beyond the scope of just sexual activity. They include jokes, innuendoes, gestures, and so on, that are of a sexual nature.
- **Intellectual:** How are my thoughts and ideas received? Are they considered? Respected? Am I provided access to information and learning?

To the unaccustomed, setting and maintaining boundaries may feel risky (and the risk of losing the relationship does, in fact, exist, because many not-so-healthy folks tend to take umbrage to having any type of boundary enforced). It is, however, a risk worth taking, because ***personal boundaries discourage abuse and exploitation, encourage contact, and lead to stronger,*** *healthier relationships.* (It's interesting that so many people fear that they will be abandoned if they attempt to set and maintain personal boundaries within relationships. I say *interesting*, because it is often **not the people who set boundaries** or **respect those boundaries**, but **the people who do not set explicit boundaries** who wind up resentful and eventually withdraw from relationships.

Recognizing, Maintaining, and Respecting Boundaries

GROUP EXERCISE

PART ONE:

Distribute both worksheets:

1. *About This Relationship*
2. *Boundary Exercise Questionnaire*

Once everyone has completed the worksheet *About This Relationship,* have participants break up into pairs. Instruct pairs to discuss their worksheet answers with regard to any to difficulties, surprises, etc. Once the worksheet has been processed in pairs, have participants return to larger group. Process within the larger group.

PART TWO:

With participants still in pairs, instruct each pair to stand approximately 20 feet apart on opposite sides of the room. Designate one line as *Movers* and one line as *Maintainers.*

Instruct the *Movers* to walk toward their partner in the *Maintainers* line until his/her partner commands him/her to stop.

Instruct the *Maintainers* to allow their partners to come as close as their physical boundary will allow. When each of the partners in the *Movers* line reaches the *Maintainers* personal comfort zone, the *Maintainer* should put his/her hand up, palm forward, and command the *Mover* by calling out, "Stop!" Once the command is given, the *Mover* should freeze in place.

Switch roles and repeat the exercise.

Once everyone has had the opportunity to be both a *Mover* and *Maintainer,* have participants return to the larger group and fill out the questionnaire.

Process participants' answers in the larger group setting.

WORKSHEET: BOUNDARIES

Healthy family functioning is characterized by emotional boundaries between individuals and subsystems that are permeable, but clear, whereas in clinical families, boundaries may be rigid, diffuse, or misaligned.

> **Rigid boundaries** tend to be associated with *disengaged families*, where members are *psychologically distant* from one another.
>
> **Blurred and/or unclear boundaries** tend to be associated with *enmeshed families* and involve an unhealthy amount of closeness and intensity between family members.

The two extremes, *disengaged* or *enmeshed* family systems, lead to considerable "boundary issues" in adult relationships. *Disengaged* families with rigid boundaries make it difficult for others to get close to them, while *enmeshed* families, with weak boundaries, tend toward overinvolvement with others, along with the sense of surrendering one's own identity in the process.

INSTRUCTIONS:

Part One: Choose one of your parents (or primary caregivers) and answer the following questions:

In what ways was your parent *distant or withdrawn* from you?

Include:

- Incidents in which you ran to your parent with enthusiasm and (s)he turned you away without following up on your excitement.
- Events missed.
- Broken promises.
- Evidence that your preferences were unknown.
- Evidence that your thought processes were not understood.
- Evidence that your interests were missed.
- Being passed over when something concerned the whole family.

In what ways was your parent *enmeshed* with you?

Include:

- Ideas held by the parent that were forced on you.
- Preferences that a parent expected you to share.
- Evidence that your parent assumed you felt the way (s)he did.
- Parental ways you were expected to adopt.

In what ways did your parent use you to meet his/her needs?

Include the need for:

- Power
- Comfort
- Sex
- Stress relief
- Solution of adult problems
- Other

Part Two: Repeat this exercise with any other caretaker who assumed a parental role toward you.

Part Three: From what you know of your grandparents on both sides, what's your best guess about their boundaries? Write about each grandparent. Identify suspected patterns of enmeshment, withdrawal, coldness, intrusion, and the expectation that children existed to meet their needs.

WORKSHEET 1: *ABOUT THIS RELATIONSHIP*

This worksheet is designed to encourage the development of relational boundaries within relationships. Choose one of your current relationships. With regard to that relationship, complete the following set of questions:

1. What type of relationship is it?

   _____

   _____

   _____

2. Is it a time-limited relationship?

   _____

   _____

   _____

3. Is it an egalitarian or hierarchical relationship?

   _____

   _____

   _____

4. Do one or both parties initiate contact? Is that a general rule?

   _____

   _____

   _____

5. In this relationship, are there certain things that you would like to say to the other, but don't? What are they?

   _____

   _____

   _____

6. If you had the freedom, what things would you like to say to the other? What prevents you from saying these things now?

   _____

   _____

   _____

7. Do you feel that your personal boundaries are respected within this relationship? Give two examples of how they are or are not:

_____

_____

_____

8. If you were able, what changes would you institute in this relationship?

_____

_____

_____

1. While you were in the *Maintainers* line:

   How did you know when to say "Stop"?

   _____

   _____

   What did you notice in your body before, during, and after you commanded your partner to stop?

   _____

   _____

   _____

   Did you say "Stop!" at the time you thought you would?

   _____

   _____

   _____

   How did it feel to create that boundary with your partner?

   _____

   _____

   _____

   Do you recognize any similarities in your process between this exercise (setting a physical boundary) to setting an emotional boundary?

   _____

   _____

   _____

   Do you think that it is easier or harder to stay "Stop" when it involves emotions?

   _____

   _____

   _____

2. While you were in the *Movers* line:

What did you notice in your body when your *Maintainer* partner commanded you to "Stop"?

_____

_____

_____

How did it feel to respect someone's boundaries?

_____

_____

_____

Based on your relationship with your *Maintainer* partner, did you expect to be allowed as close or closer than you were?

_____

_____

_____

Were you comfortable with the boundary that your partner established?

_____

_____

_____

WORKSHEET: THE MANY ROLES PLAYED

Individual or Group

"Role playing is prior to the emergence of the self. Roles do not emerge from the self, but the self may emerge from roles."

~Jay Moreno

Think about your behavior and roles in the past and present as a member of important groups throughout your life. Write down your responses regarding your role in each of the following groups:

FAMILY OF ORIGIN:

What role do you play in the family?

_____

_____

_____

_____

Why do you play this role?

_____

_____

_____

_____

What behaviors are associated with this role?

_____

_____

_____

_____

What do you feel you are/were able to say/do/feel in this role and what feels/felt unacceptable?

_____

_____

_____

_____

Has your role changed in any significant way? (Explain how and why.)

_____

_____

_____

_____

As your role changed over time, are/were you aware of any patterns that may have emerged?

_____

_____

_____

_____

SOCIAL GROUPS:

What role do you play in your social group?

_____

_____

_____

_____

Why do you play this role?

_____

_____

_____

_____

What behaviors are associated with this role?

_____

_____

_____

_____

What do you feel you are able to say/do/feel in this role and what feels unacceptable?

_____

_____

_____

_____

Has your role changed in any significant way? (Explain how and why.)

_____

_____

_____

_____

As your role has changed over time, are you aware of any patterns that may have emerged?

_____

_____

_____

_____

FRIENDSHIP GROUPS:

What role do you play in important friendships?

_____

_____

_____

Why do you play this role?

_____

_____

_____

_____

What behaviors are associated with this role?

_____

_____

_____

_____

What do you feel you are able to say/do/feel in this role and what feels unacceptable?

_____

_____

_____

_____

Has your role changed in any significant way? (Explain how and why.)

_____

_____

_____

_____

As your role has changed over time, are you aware of any patterns that may have emerged?

_____

_____

_____

_____

WORK GROUPS:
What role do you play in your work group?

_____

_____

_____

_____

Why do you play this role?

_____

_____

_____

_____

What behaviors are associated with this role?

_____

_____

_____

_____

What do you feel you are able to say/do/feel in this role and what feels unacceptable?

_____

_____

_____

_____

Has your role changed in any significant way? (Explain how and why)

_____

_____

_____

_____

As your role has changed over time, are you aware of any patterns that may have emerged?

_____

_____

_____

_____

OTHER SIGNIFICANT GROUPS

(e.g., sports teams, military experience, group therapy)

What role do you play in this group?

_____

_____

_____

_____

Why do you play this role?

_____

_____

_____

_____

What behaviors are associated with this role?

_____

_____

_____

_____

What do you feel you are able to say/do/feel in this role and what feels unacceptable?

_____

_____

_____

_____

Has your role changed in any significant way? (Explain how and why.)

_____

_____

_____

_____

As your role has changed over time, are you aware of any patterns that may have emerged?

_____

_____

_____

_____

Questions to consider regarding your responses:

1. Do you think that other members of your groups would agree with your assessment of your roles?
2. Do you recognize patterns across groups?
3. How are your roles similar/different in each group?
4. Why do you think they are similar/different?
5. Were you surprised by any of your answers?

WORKSHEET: IMPLICIT CHILDHOOD MESSAGES

Think back to your childhood.

What messages or instructions were part of your daily life?

_____

_____

_____

_____

What messages did you receive about your body?

_____

_____

_____

_____

What messages did you receive about honesty?

_____

_____

_____

_____

What messages did you receive about morality?

_____

_____

_____

_____

What messages did you receive about sex?

_____

_____

_____

_____

Now reflect on how many of these early instructions you still follow.

Have you freely chosen these instructions as an adult, or do you just live by some of them without question?

_____

_____

_____

_____

Do any of these instructions presently warrant further review?

_____

_____

_____

_____

Projection Exercise

INDIVIDUAL OR GROUP

Instructions: Picture yourself at the movie theater. Be aware that the image on the screen isn't coming from the screen, but from the projector behind you. In essence, this scenario describes the psychological process of projection, in which an attitude, trait, or quality is attributed or assigned to a person, group, or object by another—and is subsequently disowned by the projector. Simply stated, *projection is seeing in others what is present in yourself.*

This exercise can be done alone or in pairs. In the solo version, you will need an actual mirror. In the pairs version, you will need a partner.

SOLO VERSION

Write the name of a character (either from fiction or real life) whose qualities you admire.

_____

Now list the admirable qualities:

1. _____
2. _____
3. _____
4. _____
5. _____
6. _____

Turning toward the mirror, try to sustain as much eye contact as possible as you simultaneously attend to your own breathing. Begin to read aloud the list of qualities you have made. However, instead of reading only the words that you have written, you will be trying these qualities on, that is, owning each of them. For each quality you will begin with direct "I am ..." statements.

Notice any bodily sensations, thoughts, or feelings that arise as you make each statement. (Notice any resistance that arises or temptation to stop or rush through the exercise.)

The strongest reaction I had was:

_____

_____

_____

What surprised me most was:

_____

_____

_____

Transference Exercise

INDIVIDUAL OR GROUP

"We don't see things as they are; we see things as we are."

~ Anais Nin

At the conclusion of this exercise, distribute the **Attachment Patterns Worksheet**. After completing the worksheet, facilitate a discussion regarding adult attachment patterns.

Instructions: Begin by conjuring up an image of your boyfriend/girlfriend, or husband/wife, or a close friend. Now bring to mind some aspect of their personality to which you have a strong reaction—positive or negative.

Write down your reaction on a piece of paper.

Now describe in some detail that aspect (or those aspects) of his/her personality and your reaction to them. Write down the thoughts you have while experiencing that part of him/her. Write down your feelings toward that part of him/her. Write down how you behave in reaction to that part.

Now, draw a box around what you just wrote.

Write at the top of the box, "Is this transference?"

Next, conjure up an image of your parents.

Is the personality characteristic of the person that you wrote about, along with your reaction to it reminiscent of—or in some way similar to—your relationship with one (or both) of your parents? For example, does either parent share a particular personality trait that you react to so strongly?

Transference may be more tricky than simply reacting to others the way you reacted to your parent(s). Here are several possibilities:

- You see the other in the same way as you believed your parent to have been (simple transference).
- You see the other as being like what you WISH your parent COULD have been like.
- You see the OTHER AS YOU were as a child and you act as your parent did.
- You see the other as you were as a child and you act like you WISHED your parent could have acted.

GESTALT THERAPY

Gestalt Interventions

Individual and Group

According to Joel Latner (*The Gestalt Therapy Book*, 1973 pp. 123–124):

> Therapy is a safe emergency. It is safe because it is structured with the patient's interests in mind, because it is not the real-life danger. . . .
>
> It is an emergency because its experimental orientation requires that what occurs in therapy is both within the range of possibility for the patient, and also real and challenging enough to arouse the conflicts that make his present life situation untenable
>
> Experiments are not tasks. Their point is not to get them done. They exist in Gestalt therapeutic work to provide present information about the patient: What happens if you do this, or that? The importance of experiments is in how they permit us to examine what we do, and to find out what we will not do. What we will not do is our resistance, our reluctance or felt inability to carry out experiments. Seen in this way, our resistances serve as much of the stuff of the therapy, for they are expressions of how we hold ourself back.
>
> In the experiment, the patient permits his organismic self-regulation to begin to try to operate in the safety of the therapeutic situation.
>
> In skillful therapy, the experiments are ordered so that every trail brings both successes and new resistance. Each experiment has within it the potential for coming to grips with an aspect of our self-conquest in a setting where we may again begin to assert the predominance of our present satisfaction over outmoded ways of being. Action leads to feeling, feeling to understanding. In the experiment, we come to know what we do, and, in the process, we discover new paths.

I owe a debt of gratitude to Frederick S. Perls, Ralph F. Hefferline, and Paul Goodman, as most—if not all—of the following interventions owe their origin to their timeless text, ***Gestalt Therapy: Excitement and Growth in the Human Personality*** (1972, 1951) (okay, so maybe not timeless).

In my relatively short career, I have been extraordinarily blessed and unbelievably lucky to have worked with so many talented Gestalt therapists; I remain indebted to each. In my personal and professional development, I have witnessed and/or experienced each of the following interventions and was—and continue to be—amazed by not only their power, but their sheer simplicity. (Again, *simple* should in no way connote that they are *easy*.)

Read over the following Gestalt experiments. Imagine when and with whom you might attempt them. If you feel so inclined, make them your own.

If and when you implement an experiment, closely monitor its effects on both the client and the therapeutic relationship. Be sure to encourage the client to remain mindful throughout the experiencing phase and reflective throughout the processing phase. Without such a stance, they're really just activities.

GESTALT EXPERIMENTS

1. How is the distance between us? Can we move our chairs a bit closer to make this large group more intimate?

2. I notice that when I challenge you, you seem to stop breathing? Do you notice that? How might you remind yourself to keep breathing?

3. You've said too much for me. I'm unable to take in this much information at once. Can we slow this down a bit?

4. Are you angry with me?

5. I'm in danger of losing focus; I'm feeling overinformed by information.

6. In this group setting what catches your eye? Does a certain voice stand out for you?

7. What do you expect of me—both relationally and practically?

8. If you were getting your needs met, what would that look like?

9. Is there something you want or need from me right now?

10. Would you like to know my reaction to what you've just said?

11. Having identified that you are lonely, what strategies might you employ to seek out and include more people in your life?

12. Where do you feel that loneliness in your body?

13. If that part of you had a voice, what would it say now?

14. What do you like about me?

15. What do you dislike about me?

16. What are some of the things that I could do or say that might make you angry with me?

17. If I were to piss you off, how would I know that I'd done so?

18. If you knew that you'd die tomorrow, what would you miss?

19. If you remain in eye contact with me what—if anything—changes within you?

20. Just now, I noticed the color in your face change. (Alternatively: I notice that your face now has less/more color.) Did you notice something as well?

21. Your body appears expectant. Are you aware of wanting something from me?

22. I'm feeling tired and bored. How are you?

23. What's it like when you sit back in the chair and allow it to support you?

24. What's it like when you sit up and elongate your backbone?

25. Would you say "No" again, but this time would you push your hands up against mine? Does your experience change? In what way?

26. Scan through your body. Notice where in your body you feel the most aliveness—the most energy. Notice where in your body you feel most connected. Notice where in your body you feel least the aliveness—the least energy. Notice where in your body you feel most/least connected.

27. I notice that when you say "No," you seem to set your jaw. Do you notice that?

28. You say you feel "shaky." Would it be okay to stand up and let your body shake out some tension?

29. Let's stand up and move away from one another, leaving maybe 15 feet between us. You begin slowly walking toward me, while paying attention to your internal experience. After each step, pause and check in, noticing any sensations of activation or shutdown. Let's find the distance where you feel the most comfortable.

30. Let's stand up and move away from one another, leaving maybe 15 feet between us. You begin slowly walking toward me, while paying attention to your internal experience. After each step, pause and check in, noticing any sensations of activation or shutdown. At some point as you continue to walk toward me, I will say "Stop!" When I do, I'd like you to notice what you feel and where in your body you feel the most impact.

31. Let's stand up and move away from one another, leaving maybe 15 feet between us. I will begin slowly walking toward you. Pay attention to your internal experience. As I continue to walk toward you, you will pick a time to say "Stop!" As you do, notice what happens in your body. Notice where in your body you feel the most impact.

32. Let's stand up and move away from one another, leaving maybe 15 feet between us. I will begin slowly walking toward you. Pay attention to your internal experience. At some point as I continue to walk toward you, you will say "Stop!" Only this time, as you command me to stop, try to plant your feet firmly and hold both hands up and out. As you do, notice what happens in your body. Notice where in your body you feel the most impact.

33. When you speak, I notice that your gaze is averted. Do you notice yourself avoiding eye contact?

34. How is it for you when you remain in eye contact with me and we continue to dialogue?

35. What does your body need right now?

36. Are you willing to shake your shoulders and stretch before we attempt this again?

37. Bring up a memory of a time when you were sad. What, if any, physical reactions emerge?

38. Look around and describe in detail everything you are seeing and hearing and sensing now.

39. Scan your body and say, "Right now I am aware of. . . ."

40. Would you try moving your chair closer to mine? Is there a difference?

41. What do you need to work on before you leave today?

42. To explore your moment-to-moment awareness, just describe whatever you are hearing, seeing, or sensing in your body now.

43. I notice you touch, (hold, grip, stroke, etc.) your throat when speaking. Could you exaggerate this and see what happens?

44. What do you need to work on before returning home?

45. So what ground rules do you want to operate by?

46. In this group, who do you feel closest to and further away from?

47. You look detached from the group—are you?

48. Have we, as a group, developed sufficiently clear rules and boundaries for you to feel safe?

49. What do you think is permitted here, and what do you see as forbidden?

50. Is something I am doing holding us back?

51. What do you distrust most about me as a group leader/therapist?

52. Who or what maintains the boundaries here?

53. Tell me what you most appreciate about yourself.

54. You've spoken about feeling less than or not good enough. Would you be willing to experiment with a little bit of bragging?

55. If I were _____, what might you say to me to move this situation on?

56. What might you need to say to _____ next time you meet to complete this issue?

57. How might you develop support to meet _____ from a more empowered position?

58. Try completing 10 sentences starting, "I really like the way I. . . ."

59. Is there a statement behind your question?

60. Do you have a specific issue you'd like to work on today?

61. What do you need from this group right now?

62. If you felt supported, what might that look like?

63. What might you be willing to sacrifice to free up some time and energy to devote to this relationship?

64. What is it like when you change "*I have to . . .*" to "*I choose to . . .*"?

65. If you woke up tomorrow and your life was perfect, what would have happened overnight?

66. You seem to find taking in praise much more difficult than taking in criticism. Does that assessment fit?

67. What criticisms of me—if any—are you aware of at this moment?

68. Can you foresee any issues that might cause a rift between us?

69. If you were my therapist, what would you suggest I work on?

70. What emotions are informing and motivating you right now?

71. How did you feel when I said _____?

72. Do certain words tend to trigger negative emotions in you?

73. Is there someone that I remind you of?

74. I'm feeling emotionally drained. Where are you?

75. I don't like the aggression I experience in this setting.

76. I notice feeling angry, although I can't figure why. Are you experiencing something similar?

77. How would it be for you to exaggerate that emotion, raise your voice, and stand up? Would you be willing to try that?

78. I notice that you just said something that seems painful, yet you are still smiling. Do you notice that?

79. As an experiment, are you willing to say that again, but this time with your chest a bit more open and perhaps, not smiling, just to see if you experience it differently?

80. Are you willing to put yourself into a posture that best expresses that emotion (fear, anger, terror, joy. . .)?

81. Although your voice is soft, I suspect that you are angry. Would you be willing to make a fist and shake it to make your point?

82. While expressing your anger, would you be willing to squeeze, pound, or shake this pillow? As you do that, what sound or noise might go with those movements?

83. What is it like to say "won't" in place of "can't"?

84. Does anyone in this group remind you of one or both of parents?

85. If I were your mother, what unexpressed feelings might you share with me?

86. How do you stop yourself from expressing anger?

87. Some people bite the inside of their cheek or dig their nails into their skin; how do you physically stop yourself from crying (or from expressing any other emotion)?

88. If you weren't laughing, how else might you express your feelings right now?

89. Imagine yourself five years old, waking up in your bedroom. What do you see?

90. Which emotion are you the most familiar or comfortable with?

91. When you drift off or *space out*, where do you generally go?

92. How are you different in this group from the way you are outside of this group? What accounts for those differences?

93. I appreciate your "No."

94. I like my provocative (mischievous, introspective, etc.) nature, which I see reflected in you.

95. What words come to mind when you look at me?

96. If you sat opposite yourself as a 10-year-old and asked him/her to advise you, what do you imagine (s)he might say?

97. Imagine standing on a beach looking out over the ocean. A small rowboat approaches the shore. You see a figure approaching, carrying a small box, which is left for you to open. Inside the box is a message for you. What does this message say?

98. Are you willing to play the part of your father/mother/sibling/spouse so that I might interview him/her to learn about his/her relationship with you?

99. What creative risks might you take in your life?

100. When you sit opposite me and look into my eyes, what comes up for you that might interfere with our meeting (making contact)?

101. Is there something I should know that would help me to fully appreciate who you are?

102. Some people say that we choose our parents. If that were true (and pretend that it is), why did you choose yours?

103. When you feel the most loving, where are you? Is anybody with you?

104. If you were a profoundly wise (wo)man—what advice would you give me?

Many believe *The Empty Chair* experiment to be synonymous with Gestalt therapy. Obviously, that's nonsense! Because you most likely know it, you might as well use it. Here's the gist of it.

THE EMPTY CHAIR

INSTRUCTIONS:

1. Invite the participant to set up two chairs facing each other.

2. Inform the participant that the chair will be representative of whatever (s)he wishes to put in it; a *part of him/herself*, a person, drug of choice, a problematic behavior, etc.

3. Once the participant has chosen what or who will go in the chair, invite him/her to begin by saying whatever (s)he needs to say to whom/what the chair represents.

4. Role reversal should be employed throughout (i.e., whatever is in the chair is given a voice). During this *role reversal*, the protagonist switches chairs and acts the part for a minute or two.

5. The scene plays out in this way until completion (i.e., the protagonist feels finished).

6. At that point the facilitator/director instructs him/her with: "Say the last thing you need to say," and then calls for quiet.

7. After a quiet pause, processing begins.

8. The facilitator/director may ask the protagonist specific questions regarding his/her internal experiences (i.e., body sensations, emotions, thoughts, memories, insights, etc.).

9. Finally, the facilitator/director invites the audience (those in the group who were not directly involved in the scene) to provide feedback to the protagonist regarding his/her feelings with respect to the scene. Prompts such as "How does what you've witnessed or been a part of relate to something in your own life?" may be offered to clarify the type of feedback that is being solicited.

PSYCHODRAMA

Role Playing

"Role playing is prior to the emergence of the self. Roles do not emerge from the self, but the self may emerge from roles."

~Jay Moreno

This next set of exercises comes to you from Moreno's world of psychodrama.

The structure of a typical psychodrama group is developed through the use of sociometric (sociometry = the science of social connections) exercises, which provide awareness to the group regarding its members' commonalties that in turn build trust, rapport, and respect. Psychodrama groups are typically brief, solution-focused, and tend to address participants' core issues and, therefore, are often intense. Each psychodrama session runs approximately 1½ to 3 hours.

The following description of a typical psychodrama session is followed by exercises borrowed from this modality:

1. A set of warm-up exercises.

2. Negotiation between the group regarding choosing a "protagonist" (i.e., who will "work" during the session).

3. With input from the group, the facilitator/director picks a group member who is ready and willing to work on one of his/ her personal problems.

4. The group leader asks the protagonist to briefly state his/ her problems. (This statement should be limited to a few sentences.)

5. The leader immediately moves the protagonist from this narrative phase into a "scene" that is relevant to and representative of his/her problem.

6. The protagonist is instructed to choose members from the group to play roles in this scene. (The roles cast are customarily those of significant people in the protagonist's life.) The group members who are chosen are instructed to do their best to portray the given role, usually without further clarification.

7. Sometimes the protagonist requires a "double." The double may be chosen prior to the beginning of a scene or during a scene if it becomes apparent that the protagonist is unable to bring out all (s)he needs to, is blocking emotion or expression, or is unable to verbalize his/her feelings. The facilitator/director will either (a) instruct the protagonist to choose a double to come and speak for and through him/her, or (b) designate a double without input from the protagonist. Schützenberger gives this description of the double's assignment:

From a technical point of view the <u>double, B,</u> stands or sits to one side of and a little bit behind the protagonist, A. The <u>double</u> puts into words the feelings she/he is aware of in the *protagonist, A, or that she/ he guesses to be there, and which the protagonist fails to express, out of shyness, inhibition, pain, guilt, aggression, politeness . . . or because she/he is unaware of feeling them or doesn't know how to put them into words. The <u>double's</u> job is to give form to and to make conscious to the protagonist his/her preconscious feelings, and, if need be, help the psychodramatist to guide the protagonist onto a path that seems useful. . . . The protagonist has the full right to disown and repudiate the double's verbalizations at any time.*

8. The facilitator/director calls for action, and the scene begins.

9. At certain points during the scene, the group leader should inquire about the accuracy of the roles being played. If on target, the scene continues uninterrupted. If not, the facilitator/director instructs the protagonist to *switch roles* with the group member playing that role. During this *role reversal*, the protagonist acts the part for a minute or two, thereby defining the role for the group member playing that role. This sequence is repeated as necessary, ensuring that all the actors in the protagonist's scene get to know their parts.

10. The scene plays out in this way until completion (i.e., the protagonist feels finished. At that point the facilitator/director calls for quiet.

11. After a quiet pause, processing begins.

12. The protagonist is invited to describe his/her feelings while (s)he was acting and/or observing different parts of the scene. The facilitator/director may ask specific questions regarding his/her internal experiences (i.e., body sensations, emotions, thoughts, memories, insights, etc.).

13. The facilitator/director should move on to the participants who played the various roles. Each participant is invited to share thoughts and feelings related to playing their respective roles.

14. The facilitator/director debriefs all the participants/actors. Among the many ways to do this debriefing, it is recommended that each person who played a role should in some manner address the protagonist with what may seem (but is often not) an obvious statement asserting who (s)he is and who (s)he is not (e.g., *"I'm not your mother, I'm your friend, Diane." "I'm not your brother, I'm Kenny."*).

Finally, the facilitator/director invites the audience (those in the group who were not directly involved in the scene) to provide feedback to the protagonist regarding his/her feelings about the scene. Prompts such as "How does what you've witnessed or been a part of relate to something in your own life?" may be offered to clarify the type of feedback that is being solicited.

Warm-up Exercises: Sociometry

GROUP

INSTRUCTIONS:

The facilitator gives the following instructions to the group:

Choose someone here that you would like to know. Walk over to that person and introduce yourself. After participants have paired up, have them answer the following questions:

1. What was it like to be chosen?
2. What was it like to be the chooser?
3. Was that a familiar role?
4. Are you satisfied with that role?

Now, one participant will interview the other for one minute, noting verbal and nonverbal communication. After the interview, the interviewer will try to show his/her partner how the partner appeared to him/her. Then, answer the following questions:

1. What is it like being the other person?
2. What is it like seeing yourself?
3. Is there something about yourself you would like to understand better or to change?

A Message for You

INDIVIDUAL OR GROUP

INSTRUCTIONS:

Facilitator gives the following instructions to the group:

GUIDED IMAGERY SCRIPT

Begin by sitting comfortably with your back, neck, and spine fully supported. Gently close your eyes. Now begin to bring your attention to your breath—the direct experience of your breath—however it is . . . and however it changes. You may wish to close your eyes for this imagery, however if you'd rather not, just choose a spot to focus your gaze where you won't be easily distracted.

Now bring to mind the image of a plain white envelope. It is addressed to and has been delivered to you. As you unfold the paper you immediately recognize the handwriting. You begin to read the letter, taking all the time you need. When you have read it all, slowly return to the room.

- Who was the letter from?
- What was the message from this person?

Writing Your Own Eulogy

GROUP

INSTRUCTIONS:

1. Ask participants to imagine that they died today.

2. Instruct participants to write the eulogy that they would like to have read during their own funeral.

3. Give participants adequate time to both imagine their death and to sit quietly writing their eulogy.

4. When the group comes back together, invite participants to share their experience of thinking and writing about both their life and death.

5. Invite each person to share his/her eulogy with the rest of the group.

Representing Feelings

GROUP

INSTRUCTIONS:

The facilitator asks participants to "choose something in the room that represents how you are feeling now."

Give some time for each participant to identify something.

During the first go-round, invite each participant to tell the group what (s)he has chosen. (If a participant is unable to identify something, ask them how they feel and allow the group to suggest some ideas.)

After each participant has identified what (s)he has chosen, go around again, allowing each to elaborate on what (s)he chose, why (s)he chose it, and what feeling it represents.

During this go-round, the facilitator should draw out group members, helping them to identify possible issues to which this feeling(s) may be related.

Identify and discuss any commonalities or themes within the group.

The Best Gift Ever Given/Received

GROUP

This two-part exercise deals with giving and receiving

INSTRUCTIONS:

PART ONE:

The facilitator brings in a gift-wrapped box, places it prominently on display, and begins by drawing attention to the box. The facilitator then asks participants to recall in their imagination the best gift they have ever received. Allow time for the memory to become vivid in all its dimensions. Instruct the group to pay attention not only to the gift, but to their sensory experience while experiencing the memory of the gift.

On the first go-round, the facilitator asks each participant to identify just how they feel presently, without sharing any information about the gift.

On the next go-round, each participant is asked to identify the following:

- What and why (s)he felt as (s)he did
- What the gift meant to him/her
- Who gave the gift
- What it was like to receive the gift

PART TWO:

The facilitator asks participants to once again close their eyes and recall in their imagination the best gift they have ever given. Again, allow ample time for the memory to become vivid in all its dimensions. Instruct the group to pay attention to just the gift—what it feels like knowing (s)he will be giving it—and then to the act of giving the gift. Pay specific attention to the receiver's reaction, along with the participant's sensory and emotional experience during the memory.

On the first go-round, the facilitator asks each participant identify the following:

- Who the gift was for
- Why it was so special
- How (s)he felt at the time (s)he was giving the gift
- How (s)he feels presently

Finally, ask each participant to contrast the two experiences.

Family Sculpting Exercise

FAMILY OF THE SUBSTANCE ABUSER (GROUP)

This family sculpting technique introduced by experiential family therapists David Kantor, Fred Duhl, and Bunny Duhl was further developed by legendary psychotherapist and author, Virginia Satir.

INSTRUCTIONS:

The facilitator asks for a volunteer to develop his/her own family sculpture. The volunteer should be one who has grown up in a home in which one or both parents abused drugs or alcohol. The facilitator asks the participant to describe his/her family as a unit, and then to describe each individual's role in the family. Using this description, the family constellation will be "sculpted," with participants taking the roles of family members.

The facilitator calls for volunteers to participate in the sculpture, then assigns each participant one of the following positions:

1. Choosing participants to fill roles of family members. First, the volunteer is instructed to select a participant to play the role of his substance-abusing parent. Supporting roles (other parent, siblings, grandparents, aunts, uncles, or any other significant members of the family) are then chosen. Next, the volunteer chooses a participant to play his/her role in the family.

2. Next, the volunteer will assign physical positions within the sculpture based on:
   - *Power/Influence*
   - *Emotional Closeness*

Power/Influence: Each participant will be placed in a position commensurate with his/her power or influence within the family system. For example, if the substance-abusing parent was in a position of power then (s)he will be asked to stand on a chair to convey that level of power. Other members of the family are subsequently assigned positions corresponding to their degree of power and influence within the system (i.e., sitting on the floor, sitting on a chair, standing, or standing on a chair, etc.).

Emotional Closeness: The volunteer will then guide each participant nearer or farther from one another—facing toward or away from one another—based on the degree of emotional closeness/distance that each family member felt.

Verbal Message: The volunteer will provide each family member one spoken line to represent what that member may recall from the past. The volunteer should instruct the participant on the inflection of the line (i.e., what *feeling* is being conveyed). The line can be directed at any or all of the other family members.

Behavior Message: The volunteer will provide each family member with an action that may or may not coincide with his/her verbal message (e.g., crying, screaming, waving fists, pointing fingers, stamping of the feet, etc.).

. . . And Action: Once each of the participants has an understanding his/her respective roles, including the verbal and behavioral messages, the facilitator gives the signal to begin in unison and with great emotion to recite their lines and express the actions, while the volunteer and the facilitator watch as the family sculpture comes to life. The action portion of the sculpture may last for several minutes until the facilitator calls for quiet.

Processing: After a quiet pause, the volunteer/observer is asked to describe his/her feelings while watching the sculpted family in action. The facilitator may ask specific questions regarding his/her internal experiences (i.e., body sensations, emotions, thoughts, memories, insights, etc.).

Once the volunteer feels finished (or expresses a desire to stop), the facilitator should move on to the participants who played the various family members. Each participant is invited to share thoughts and feelings related to playing their respective roles.

Using a prompt such as "How does what you've witnessed or been a part of relate to something in your own life?" the audience is invited to provide feedback regarding feelings about the scene.

DEBRIEFING

Once fully processed, it is important to debrief all those involved in the sculpture. The debriefing may be done in many ways, but it is recommended that each "family member" address the volunteer with what may seem (but is often not) an obvious statement asserting who (s)he is and who (s)he is not (e.g., *"I'm not your mother, I'm your friend, Diane." "I'm not your brother, I'm Kenny."*).

Guided Imagery for the Substance Abuser

GROUP

The following is related to the **Family Sculpting Exercise,** but this one is to be done by the substance abuser him/herself.

GUIDED IMAGERY SCRIPT

Begin by sitting comfortably with your back, neck, and spine fully supported. Gently close your eyes. Now begin to bring your attention to your breath—the direct experience of your breath—however it is . . . and however it changes. As you continue to pay attention to the breath, bring to mind the person who has been most negatively impacted by your addiction.

Now, imagine yourself facing that person. Take the person in fully. What are they wearing? See the shape and expression on his/her face. Notice the particular posture. Is there a familiar scent? Listen to the quality and timbre of his/her voice. What is it like to hear it now?

Begin to speak with this person. Have them speak back and to you. Listen to what (s)he is saying and how (s)he looks and sounds as (s)he continues.

Allow a few minutes for the conversation to unfold.

The facilitator ends the imagery portion and brings everybody back to the room.

On the first go-round, the facilitator instructs the processing by initially inviting each participant to report solely on who they encountered. Then on the second go-round, the facilitator invites each participant to recall and share any or all of what was said, including the emotional impact of the meeting.

THE BODY

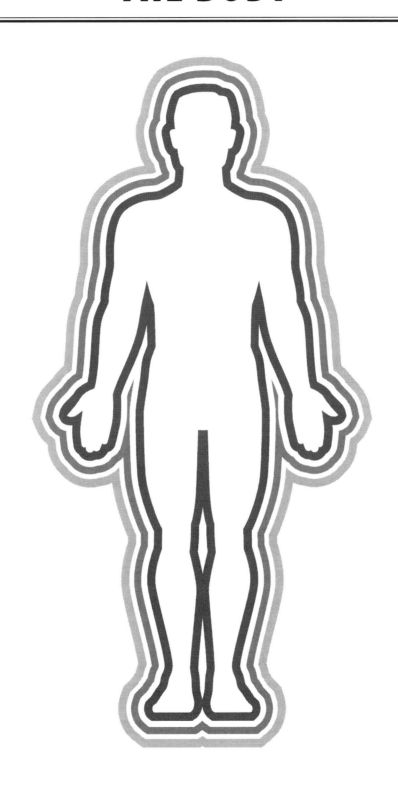

Checking In with the Body

INDIVIDUAL OR GROUP

The focusing process is based on research of Eugene Gendlin, who recognized that we all experience nascent, yet meaningful, bodily sensations for which he coined the term, *felt sense*. Gendlin posited that when these sensations were brought into conscious awareness, and attended to in a certain way, personal meaning would emerge. He subsequently developed a loose protocol to facilitate this process for which he coined the term *focusing*.

> We are all familiar with emotions, but a felt sense is not an emotion. It is a new human capacity. The felt sense of a situation or problem, when it first forms, is typically vague and unclear. You can sense that something is there, but it is hard to get it into words exactly. The felt sense is holistic in nature and contains within it much more than we can easily think or emotionally know about our situation. As the therapist and client spend time with the felt-sense, new and clearer meanings emerge.

> The felt sense, of its own accord, brings the exact word, image, memory, understanding, new idea, or action step that is needed to solve the problem. The physical body, in response, will experience some easing or release of tension as it registers the "rightness" of what comes from the felt sense. This easing of tension is what tells us that we have made contact with this deeper level of awareness and that we are on the right path. It is a body-oriented process of self-awareness and emotional healing, in which people learn to become aware of the subtle level of knowing that speaks through the body. (Cornell, 2012)

Although felt senses may occur in any area of the body, they are most often experienced in the core (abdomen, stomach, chest) or up higher in the throat. Distinct from emotions, the felt sense is better described as the feeling of the combination of sensations and emotions (e.g., if the emotion is "fear," the felt sense would contain some combination of sensations "jumpy, tense, excited, throat closing, can't speak . . ." or "deer in the headlights feeling . . . can't move"). The felt sense has an immediate here-and-now quality, transient, often vague, and not readily describable.

According to Ann Weiser Cornell Ph.D. of the Focusing Institute, the following are the *key stages of focusing*:

- "I'm sensing into my body."
- "What wants my awareness now?" or "How am I feeling about that issue?"
- "I'm saying hello to what's here."
- "I'm finding the best way to describe it."
- "I'm checking back with my body."
- "Is it OK to just be with this right now?"
- "I'm sitting with it, with interested curiosity."

- "I'm sensing how it feels from its point of view."
- "I'm asking. . . ."
- "I'm letting it know I hear it."
- I'm saying I'll be back."
- "I'm thanking my body and the parts that have been with me."

FOCUSING INSTRUCTIONS: SHORT FORM BY EUGENE GENDLIN, PH.D.

1. Clear a space

   How are you?

   What's between you and feeling fine?

   (Don't answer; let what comes in your body do the answering. Don't go into anything. Greet each concern that comes. Put each aside for a while, next to you.) Except for that, are you fine?

2. Felt sense

   Pick one problem to focus on. Don't go into the problem. What do you sense in your body when you sense the whole of that problem?

   Sense all of that, get a sense of the whole thing, the murky discomfort or the unclear body-sense of it.

3. Get a handle

   What is the quality of the felt sense? What one word, phrase, or image comes out of this felt sense? What quality-word would fit it best?

4. Resonate

   Go back and forth between word (or image) and the felt sense. Is that right? If they match, have the sensation of matching several times. If the felt sense changes, follow it with your attention. When you get a perfect match, the words (images) being just right for this feeling, let yourself feel that for a minute.

5. Ask

   What is it, about the whole problem, that makes me so _____? When stuck, ask questions:

   > What is the worst of this feeling? What's really so bad about this? What does it need? What should happen? Don't answer; wait for the feeling to stir and give you an answer. What would it feel like if it was all OK?

   Let the body answer.

   What is in the way of that?

6. Receive

   Welcome what came. Be glad it spoke. It is only one step on this problem, not the last. Now that you know where it is, you can leave it and come back to it later. Protect it from critical voices that interrupt. Does your body want another round of focusing, or is this a good stopping place?

Source: Eugene Gendlin Ph.D. (2012). The Focusing Institute. *In Carrying Life Forward Through Thought.* Retrieved 11/20/12, from http://www.focusing.org.

Note: All of the following exercises—at least in part—owe a debt to Gendlin's Focusing. To learn more about focusing visit: www.focusing.org.

Body Scan: Awareness of the Felt Sense

INDIVIDUAL OR GROUP

EXERCISES

Use the diagram on the following page. First, you will scan your body, noting your sensations on the lines next to the image.

Begin in a comfortable position—sitting or lying down. Now, breathe deeply as you focus inward. Begin with the first segment—focusing your attention and awareness on just that part of your body. (Although, most people begin at the top of the head, you should feel free to begin wherever you like. If you choose to skip any section, just note that.) After a few breaths into just that part, note what is/was present—however it is . . . and however it may have changed. Then, using the following outline, take a moment to write your awareness on the lines next to the outline.

SENSATIONS

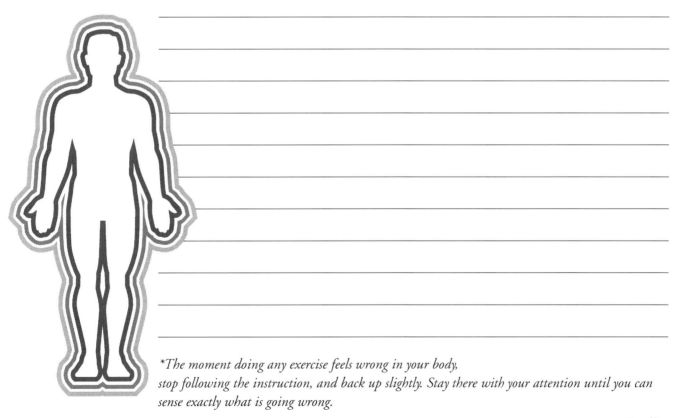

*The moment doing any exercise feels wrong in your body,
stop following the instruction, and back up slightly. Stay there with your attention until you can sense exactly what is going wrong.*

~Gendlin

Drawing Out Emotion—Awareness of the Felt Sense

The following pages present a series of emotions. Each page contains an emotion along with space for a label and a drawing. The instructions are the same for each emotion:

1. Reflect on the emotion. Try to bring up a specific incident when you experienced this emotion strongly. Allow the space for it to expand. Pay attention to the way in which you physically experience the emotion (i.e., what body sensations do you notice? Where in the body are the sensations the strongest?).

2. Using your nondominant hand, label the emotion. You may use the word or any other word or phrase that conveys its meaning for you (e.g., fear). You may write the word *FEAR* or you may want to write *afraid*, *scared to death*, etc.

3. Again, using your nondominant hand, draw a picture of the emotion. Use the colors, textures, and strokes that you feel appropriate to each emotion.

4. Reflect on the finished drawing.

On the lines provided, use your dominant hand to write out any of your observations and reactions to the drawing.

LABEL: _____

ANGER

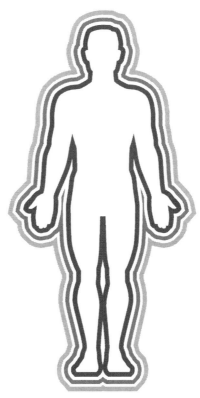

REFLECTION

_____

_____

_____

_____

_____

_____

_____

_____

LABEL: _____

SADNESS

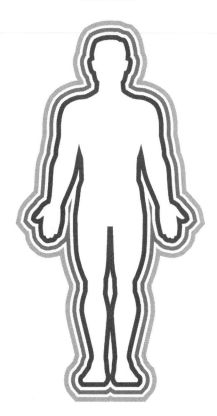

REFLECTION

_____

_____

_____

_____

_____

_____

_____

_____

_____

LABEL: _____

FEAR

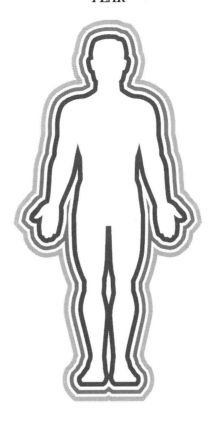

REFLECTION

_____

_____

_____

_____

_____

_____

_____

_____

LABEL: _____

TERROR

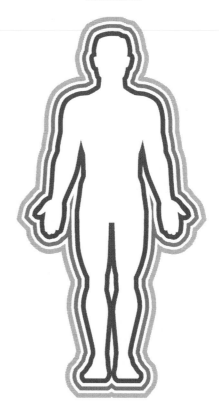

REFLECTION

_____

_____

_____

_____

_____

_____

_____

_____

LABEL: _____

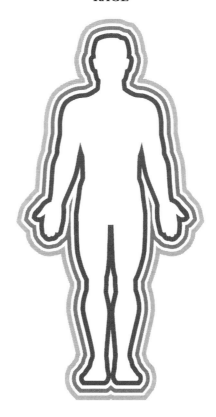

REFLECTION

_____

_____

_____

_____

_____

_____

_____

_____

LABEL: _____

CONFUSION

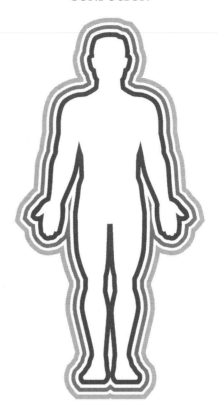

REFLECTION

_____
_____
_____
_____
_____
_____
_____
_____

LABEL: _____

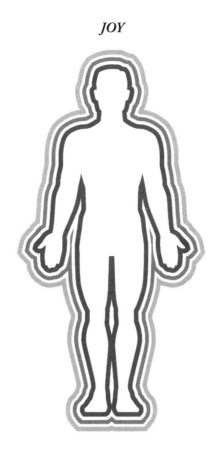

JOY

REFLECTION

_____

_____

_____

_____

_____

_____

_____

_____

LABEL: _____

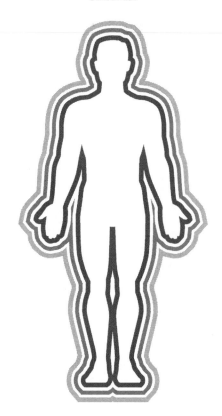

REFLECTION

_____

_____

_____

_____

_____

_____

_____

_____

LABEL: _____

SURPRISE

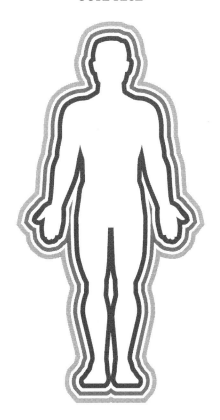

REFLECTION

_____

_____

_____

_____

_____

_____

_____

Focusing on Sensations—Awareness of the *Felt Sense*

INSTRUCTIONS:

There is no right or wrong approach to this focusing exercise; it is a process piece. Whatever you create will be right and appropriate.

EXERCISE #1

On the body map, color in the areas where you most often experience discomfort, tension, tightness, or pain. Color in the areas where you are presently experiencing discomfort, tension, tightness, or pain. Use those colors and the type of strokes that you feel best represent the particular body sensation that you are experiencing in each area of the body. For example, if you feel jittery and nervous in the stomach, you might pick a bright color and draw something that represents electricity in the stomach area. If you feel flighty and not really present, you might choose a light color and draw wispy lines wherever that sensation is noted.

Once you have completed the body map, you will be using your nondominant hand to label the colored areas with emotion word(s). Finally, on the back of the page with your dominant hand, write down any observations you have about your body map.

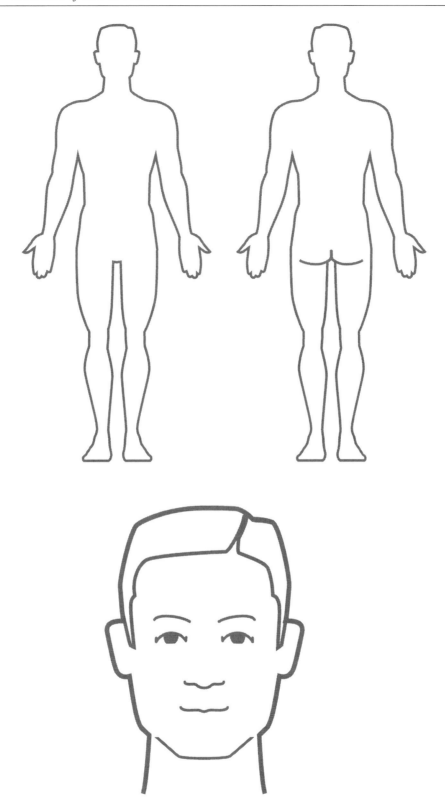

Body Scan Body Map—Awareness of the *Felt Sense*

EXERCISE 2

PART ONE:

Allow yourself to be comfortable . . . either lying down or sitting up with your back, neck, and spine fully supported. Knowing that you will not be interrupted for the next little while, begin by gently closing your eyes. Now begin to bring your attention to your breath—the direct experience of your breath—however it is . . . and however it changes. Allow yourself to softly focus your awareness on to the breath that is arising right now . . . the in-breath and the out-breath . . . the rising and the falling. If you can, try to follow one full cycle of the breath from the beginning of the in-breath and through its entirety the beginning of the out-breath and through its entirety. Allow yourself the time and the space to be in direct contact with the breath throughout one entire cycle. Now, starting at the crown of your head, gently guide your focus down your entire body, noticing and then noting any and all sensations. Notice any tension, tightness, and any pressure; notice any sensations of warmth, coolness, pain, or areas of numbness, feelings of softness or pleasure and relaxation. Just note what is. Continue to scan, noticing any other identifiable sensations. Allow yourself to label them, and then gently bring your attention back to the direct experience of the sensations themselves. When you've completed the journey through the entire body, bring your attention back to the room.

Using the following body map, color in all areas of the body that were calling to you—any signals of pain, pressure, tension, tightness, calm, relaxation, etc. Use those colors and the type of strokes that you feel best represent the particular body sensation that you are experiencing in each area of the body. For example, if you feel jittery and nervous in the stomach, you might pick a bright color and draw something that represents electricity in the stomach area. If you feel flighty and not really present, you might choose a light color and draw wispy lines wherever that sensation is noted.

PART TWO:

Choose the area that was signaling the loudest—the one with the strongest sensations of pain, tension, or tightness. In the outline below, mark that body area.

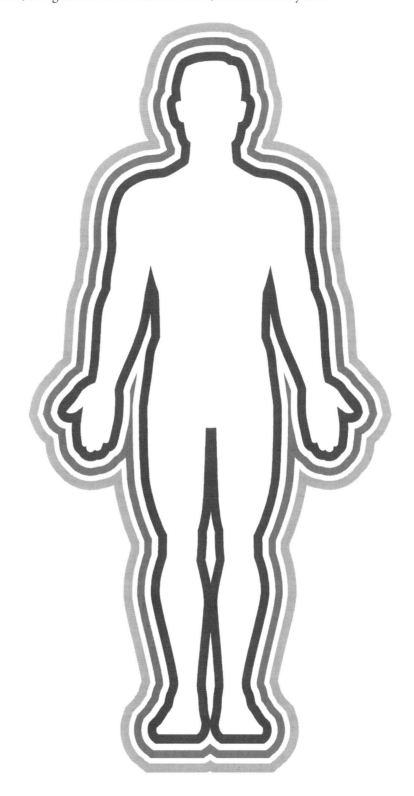

PART THREE:

In the space provided, you will be writing out a dialogue between you and that body part. You will be using both hands, therefore both hemispheres of your brain. With your dominant hand, you will write out the questions, and with your nondominant hand you will answer the questions:

- What are you?
- How are feeling?
- How long have you been feeling bad?
- What has you feeling like that?
- Is there something you want or need from me? Is there something I can do to help you?
- Is there something I need to know from you?
- Is it okay to stop now?
- Should I check in again?

DOMINANT HAND QUESTIONS	NONDOMINANT HAND ANSWERS

YOGA

Yoga

"Yoga teaches us to cure what need not be endured and endure what cannot be cured."

~B. K. S. Iyengar

"If you want to use yoga to heal emotional pain, you must find out where the pain resides in your body and learn to take your breath there. I don't teach yoga to help people to transcend. I want people's spirits to reside in their bodies. I literally want to help people embody their spirit. Not go through life fragmented."

~Ana Forrest

"Yoga cultivates your witness consciousness. It allows you to observe yourself on the mat. You aren't numbing out or going into default mode by overworking, watching TV, or reaching for the alcohol or carbs. For a trauma survivor, yoga, when practiced with awareness of breath and sensation, can be a gentle way to begin to reoccupy her body. When living in a body feels safe again, yoga postures can be used therapeutically to hold and then release the trauma stored there. Often the emotional and physical releases happen without reference to the story, so the survivor is no longer trapped in the victim role."

~Amy Weintraub

The effects of trauma are primarily physiological—leaving an indelible biological imprint. Trauma can cause an inflammatory response that leads to increased fibrosis, loss of available movement between layers, and stickiness to interstitial elements, resulting in chronic conditions of structural abnormality. Trauma disrupts clients' relationships to their bodies and emotions, leaving them feeling constricted, tense, helpless, disconnected, hurt, agitated, frantic, and in conflict with themselves, others, and the world.

By now, one can hardly doubt that state of mind and state of body are intimately related. When the mind is relaxed, the muscles relax. When stressed, a state of physical and mental tension is produced. As stated by one of the giants in mind-body medicine, Dr. Candace Pert:

> All systems of the body exchange neuropeptide information, and it is the internal feeling state (emotions) that elicits the neuropeptide response. This is the mind-body connection in which every change in the mental-emotional state causes a change in the body physiology. Likewise, every change in the body physiology causes a change in the mental-emotional state.

Although yoga takes many different forms, most Westerners already identify yoga with Hatha yoga, a yoga that seeks to promote health and well-being through physical exercise. With its profound effect on the circulation and on the functioning of the inner organs, glands, and nerves, a regular practice of asanas (postures), and breathing exercises (pranayama) makes the physical body strong, supple, and healthy. In addition, yoga offers psychological and spiritual benefits as well. Addressing the body's deep sensations and emotions, Hatha yoga helps clients to address their autonomic nervous system symptoms of hyperarousal, process their traumatic memories, and gain mastery over the posttraumatic legacy of self-doubt and despair, thus appreciably changing how they organize themselves in relation to the world and aiding in reclaiming autonomy and authority over their own lives.

The Trauma Center at Justice Resource Institute (JRI) in Massachusetts has conducted preliminary research investigating Hatha yoga's effect on some common symptomatology of PTSD. The research bears out yoga's efficacy on core physiologic parameters associated with PTSD including heart rate variability (HRV).

YOGA FOR PTSD

"An essential aspect of recovering from trauma is learning ways to calm down, or self-regulate. For thousands of years, yoga has been offered as a practice that helps one calm the mind and body. More recently, research has shown that yoga practices, including meditation, relaxation, and physical postures, can reduce autonomic sympathetic activation, muscle tension, and blood pressure, improve neuroendocrine and hormonal activity, decrease physical symptoms and emotional distress, and increase quality of life. For these reasons, yoga is a promising treatment or adjunctive therapy for addressing the cognitive, emotional, and physiological symptoms associated with trauma, and PTSD specifically."

~Excerpted from *The International Journal of Yoga Therapy*

Yoga is recognized as a form of mind-body medicine. The relaxation induced by meditation helps to stabilize the autonomic nervous system with a tendency toward either sympathetic or parasympathetic dominance. Because yoga decreases the amount of catecholamines produced by the adrenal glands during stress, it offers a host of psychological benefits. By lowering the hormone levels of the neurotransmitters norepinephrine and epinephrine, yoga produces an increased feeling of calm and well-being. Additionally, yoga is likely to reduce anxiety and depression by boosting oxygen levels to the brain.

Spiritually, a yoga practice can counter the sense of isolation often experienced by trauma clients, offering instead a sense of connection to the Divine Being or a feeling of transcendence. Yoga is the one single technique that combines and provides the benefits of breathing exercises, stretching, fitness programs, and meditation. Because it is a system for restoring balance to the body, mind, and spirit, yoga is an ideal modality for trauma clients. By working with the body and the breath in a series of postures (asanas), yoga enables them to release muscle tension, gain flexibility and strength, and quiet the mind, helping practitioners to become more resilient to stressful conditions. Yoga can also reduce the risk of developing certain diseases such as those of the cardiovascular system.

EXERCISES

What follows are some examples of posture (asana) groups with some basic instruction. Feel free to experiment. As with most things, one size does not fit all. A yoga practice should be individualized for each person. Although it's true that every posture (asana) may not be right for every person, some seem to be particularly useful to most people.

Remember, yoga should NOT BE PAINFUL!

Restorative postures are poses that aim to soothe the nervous system and release muscle tension. Examples include **Sitting/Easy Pose** and **Corpse Pose**.

Sitting/Easy Pose (*Sukhasana*) is a simple sitting pose.

This pose is a good starting position that will help to focus your awareness on to your breath and body, while strengthening your lower back and opening both the groin and hips.

1. Sit back on your heels, with hands resting on your thighs, or cross-legged with hands resting gently on your knees.

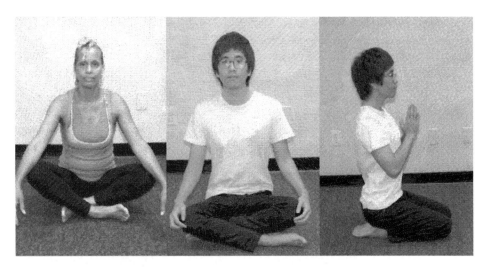

2. Focus on your breath—however it is and however it changes.
3. Keep your spine straight, while gently pushing your sit bones down into the floor.
4. If you are seated, allow your knees to gently lower toward the floor. If your knees rise above your hips, sit on a cushion or block to help support your back and hips.
5. Take a few slow, deep breaths.
6. With the next inhale, gently raise your arms over your head.

7. Exhale while bringing your arms down slowly.
8. Repeat a few times.

As with any pose, if you find it difficult or painful, feel free to try different variation(s). In this case, it's the half-lotus posture. Instead of placing both feet on the thighs, only one foot is placed on top of the opposite thigh and the other is placed under the opposite thigh. Feel free to alternate positions to allow both knees to be stretched.

SEATED NECK ROLLS

1. Begin by sitting in Easy Pose (Sukhasana).

2. Slowly allow your chin to sag gently toward your chest.

3. On the inhale, roll your left ear toward your left shoulder. On the exhale, come back to center.

4. On the inhale, roll your right ear toward your right shoulder. On the exhale, come back to center.

5. Continue slowly rolling your head from side to side for a few breaths, noticing any sensations that arise, including any tension, tightness, soreness, or numbness that may be there.

6. Notice your neck muscles as they contract and relax with the movement. Experiment with bigger or smaller movements as you continue to pay attention to the effects of each movement.

7. When you are ready, gently guide your chin back to center, lifting your head up and back to center.

Remember, yoga should NOT BE PAINFUL!

Corpse Pose (Savasana) is a resting pose (a fully present, fully aware resting pose) that provides the body the time necessary to process and integrate information at the end of the practice.

1. Begin by gently lying down on your back. Breathing deeply in and out through your nose, gently allow your feet to fall out to either side.

2. Slightly separate your arms from your body, allowing them to rest comfortably alongside your body, with your palms facing up. If that doesn't feel comfortable to you, you might try placing your arms across your chest or lying on your side.

3. If you like, allow your eyes to close.

4. Begin to bring your awareness to your breath. Allow it to be natural—however it is . . . and however it changes.

5. Let your body feel heavy as you become aware of it resting on the floor. You may wish to set a timer (from a minute to several minutes).

6. After the set period, you should begin to come out of the pose, by first beginning to deepen your breath. Take a few deep breaths, as you begin to move your fingers and toes, reawakening the body.

7. When you feel ready, bring your knees into your chest and roll over to one side, slowly bringing yourself back up into a sitting position.

8. While sitting in this way, become aware of any sensations that arise.

STANDING MOUNTAIN POSE

Standing Mountain Pose is a basic standing pose that improves posture, stability, and balance, centering the body and calming the emotions. It also serves as a starting position for all other standing poses. So take some time with this one.

1. Begin by standing with your feet shoulder-width apart, taking notice of your feet placed firmly on the ground.

2. Rest your attention on your feet, while observing anything that comes into your awareness.

3. When you are ready, begin to slowly roll your weight onto your toes, then come back down again. Observe any sensations . . . paying particular attention to the connection your toes make with the ground.

4. With your feet firmly planted on the ground, shift your awareness to the top of your head.

5. Taking a slow, deep breath, begin lifting up through your core to the top of your head. Notice this feeling—a feeling of being firmly rooted to the ground—while extending your body toward the sky. Notice any sensations or emotions that accompany this standing position.

6. With your feet planted firmly under your extended body, bring your attention to the area just below your navel.

7. Rest your awareness here—your center of gravity, your core. Remain here for a moment, noticing your center.

8. Observe any sensations or emotions that accompany this position.

9. As you inhale, imagine the breath coming up through the floor, rising through your legs and torso and up into your head.

10. Reverse the process on the exhale and watch your breath as it moves down from your head, through your chest and stomach, legs and feet.

11. Hold this standing-tall posture for 5 to 10 breaths.

Remember, yoga should NOT BE PAINFUL!

FORWARD BEND

Forward Bend is a tension-releasing pose for the back, spine, shoulders, and upper body area for increasing the flow of prana or vital life force.

1. Begin by standing with your feet shoulder-width apart, taking notice of your feet placed firmly on the ground.

2. Take a breath in, bend your knees slightly, and on the exhale, gently bend forward from the hip joints, not from the waist, allowing your hands to be dangle freely in front of you (or hold the opposite forearm), as you gently reach toward the floor. If touching the floor isn't possible, you may want to cross your forearms and hold opposite elbows.

3. Press your heels firmly into the floor and lift your sit bones toward the ceiling. Turn the top of your thighs slightly inward.

4. Notice any sensations that accompany this folded-over position. Notice where your weight is, and what happens when you shift slightly to the left, right, front, or back.

5. With each inhale, lift and lengthen the front torso just slightly; with each exhale, release a little more fully into the bend, allowing your torso to oscillate with the breath.

6. Let your head hang from the root of the neck, which is deep in the upper back, between the shoulder blades. If you like, begin to move your head slightly from side to side and/ or up and down, while taking notice of any sensations or emotions that arise.

7. When you are ready (or after a minute or so), gently and slowly begin to roll your spine up, once again coming into a standing position (Mountain Pose).

8. If you notice any tension/tightness or discomfort in your low back, place your hands on your thighs supporting yourself as you ascend.

9. Once back in Mountain Pose, allow your breath to return to "normal" while paying attention to how your body feels in this position.

Remember, yoga should NOT BE PAINFUL!

CHILD'S POSE

Child's Pose (*Balasana*) is a resting pose that happens to be a great beginning yoga pose for newcomers to yoga exercises.

1. Begin by coming down onto the floor into a kneeling position. Touch your big toes together and sit back on your heels.

2. Spread your knees about as wide as your hips.

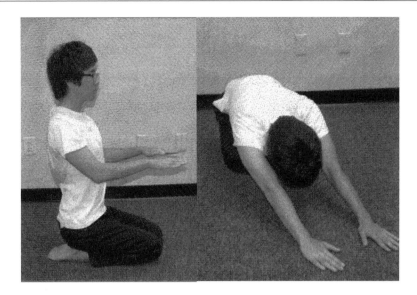

3. Exhale and lay your torso down **between** your thighs.

4. Gently stretching, lengthen your tailbone away from the back of the pelvis, while lifting the base of your skull away from the back of your neck

5. Feel how the weight of the front shoulders pulls the shoulder blades wide across your back. Remain in this pose anywhere from 30 seconds to a few minutes.

Stretch to the left, then the right. Remain in each pose anywhere from 30 seconds to a few minutes.

6. When you are ready to come up, first lengthen the front of your torso.

7. Take a slow deep breath as you lift from the tailbone as it presses down and into the pelvis.

8. Return to the starting position.

CAT TILT

Cat Tilt (*Bidalasana)* is one of the simplest, yet most beneficial of all the poses for releasing the muscles of the neck and upper back, increasing the mobility of the pelvis, and creating space in the joints of the shoulder and hips, while opening the lower back.

1. Start on your hands and knees. Position your hands directly beneath your shoulders and your knees directly beneath the hips. Spread your fingers out.

2. In this neutral position, you try to keep your back flat, spine fully extended, as you gaze toward the floor.

3. Press downward into the floor, as you begin lifting upward out of your shoulder and lengthen your arms.

4. Inhale deeply. As you exhale, tilt your hips by gently pulling the abdominal muscles backward toward the spine.

5. Tuck the tailbone (coccyx) down and under as you gently tighten the buttocks.

6. Press down firmly with your hands, while pushing the middle of your back up toward the ceiling. Round your spine upward, as you curl your head inward. Keeping your gaze on the floor.

7. Return to the starting position.

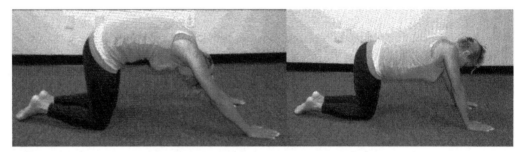

Remember, yoga should NOT BE PAINFUL!

DÖ-IN

Dö-In Exercises

INDIVIDUAL OR GROUP

INTRODUCTION

Dö means to lead or pull the Chi-energy into the body. *In* means stretching. According to Michio Kushi, the author of *Dö-In: Exercise for Physical and Spiritual Development (1979)*:

1. Dö-In has been developed from an unknown ancient time through intuitive responses, which arise without special elaboration or theories, as everyone's natural reactions of self-adjustment.

2. Dö-In is completely self-exercise, unlike many medical treatments, martial arts, and other therapies, which require the participation of other people.

3. Dö-In exercises do not require the use of any instruments, unlike acupuncture, moxibustion, and many other physiotherapies. They require only our own physical and mental functions, properly applied through self-adjustment.

4. Dö-In exercises aim toward our physical betterment and well-being, but they also aim far beyond the physical dimension toward the development of our mental and spiritual abilities for the achievement of true human nature as a whole, in all dimensions.

Dö-In exercises can be practiced anywhere at any time. Kushi has labeled each exercise according to its traditional meaning and purpose. They can be practiced as a series, but each is an independent exercise, so you should feel free to experiment with all of them, but continue with only those that are helpful to you.

TEN-DAI: HEAVENLY FOUNDATION (YANG)☯

In the beginning and at the end of each Dö-In exercise, return to a stable, grounded sitting posture. If this position causes any discomfort, sit deeply in a chair with natural straight posture, knees bent at a ninety-degree angle. Leave a space of 2–3 inches between the knees.

110

SEI-ZA: RIGHT SITTING POSTURE

Sit on the ground or the floor with natural straight posture, the muscles relaxed, including the shoulders and elbows. Leave a space of 2–3 inches between the knees.

In this position, rest your left hand atop your right, palms facing up, thumbs touching one another so that the tips of the thumbs meet. Gently relax the eyes, closing them halfway and look forward and downward. Choose a spot to rest your gaze about 10–15 feet in front of you. Then allow your eyes to relax without focusing on anything in particular. Unless otherwise stated, breathing should be done through the nose.

1. Begin with a long, deep cleansing breath. Breathing in deeply, bring the inhalation all the way down to your navel.

2. Hold the breath for several seconds, allowing the abdomen to remain expanded toward the front.

3. Exhale slowly and fully.

4. Continue for the next 3–5 minutes to focus on each breath as it arises, all the while becoming more and more stable, rooted firmly upon the earth. Picture yourself as immovable regardless of any circumstance.

AI-WA: LOVE AND HARMONY:

This exercise is centered at the Fourth Chakra, the heart and emotional center. Similar to a *Loving Kindness Meditation*, this exercise aids in the development of peaceful and cooperative relations with people and the environment.

It may be practiced alone or with an *Other*. (When practiced with another, each will gaze into the *Other's* eyes.) This exercise generates the active flow of the electromagnetic force and accelerates the circulation of blood to the heart. Additionally, this exercise produces *good vibrations* that radiate from the center of the chest area (the heart chakra).

Breathing during this exercise is through a slightly opened mouth.

1. Keep your eyes half-open, looking toward the infinite distance without focusing on any particular point. Open both arms out wide, with your hands opened naturally toward the front, as if opening for an embrace.

2. Begin to breathe deeply into the chest. Taking long, deep, but gentle inhalations, begin to direct the energy of the breath toward your heart. Continue with long, gentle inhalations, followed by slightly longer, gentle exhalations. During the inhalations, move your chest slightly forward and up; as you exhale your chest naturally returns to its resting position.

3. Repeat this breathing and the chest motion as you bring to mind the person to whom you would direct this love. Silently repeat the words *love* and *harmony* or any other word that conveys those feelings.

4. Continue this exercise for 3–5 minutes, and then return to the **Right Sitting Posture** and gradually let go of the image and word(s).

SHŌ-TEN: ASCENDING TO HEAVEN (YIN)☯

This exercise is centered at the midbrain area, the Sixth Chakra, and is said to create mental clarity. The practice of this particular exercise produces a parasympathetic response, which includes a slowing of the heart, decrease in body temperature, and a gradual loss of sensory perception. Together with the decline in physical metabolism, mental function is intensified.

Breathing during this exercise is through a slightly opened mouth.

1. Begin, seated in *Right Sitting Posture* in a quiet environment.
2. Allow yourself to relax. Open both arms in complete relaxation while keeping your eyes either lightly closed or half-opened, looking up at least 45 degrees as if you were trying to see the center of your forehead (*Third Eye*).

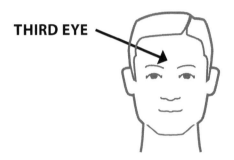

THIRD EYE

3. Gently allow all the muscles in your face to relax.
4. Breathe in through the mouth with deep, intensive inhalations, coupled with short relaxed exhalations. The exhalations are relatively passive, because the body does so naturally.
5. As you inhale, direct the breath toward the midbrain, as if the breath is passing through the center of the brain, then out and upward.
6. The deeper the inhalations, the more profound the effect.
7. Continue this exercise for 3–5 minutes. While you continue this type of breathing, you will increasingly experience your physical metabolism slowing down, your body temperature dropping, and your mouth becoming drier. Additionally, you may notice your sensory experience diminishing, as your consciousness simultaneously expands.
8. After some duration of these experiences, we gradually return to normal breathing and return both eyes to normal condition. If this exercise is intolerable or makes you unbearably cold, let go of this one.

QIGONG

Qigong

In traditional Chinese medicine, qi (pronounced "chee") is the vital life energy that flows through all living things in the universe. Traditional Chinese medicine contends that when imbalances in the flow of qi occur, or when blockages of the flow of qi through the meridian system occur, a person may suffer from illness, disease, and pain. Qigong is an ancient healing art and a regimen of slow movement exercise with controlled breathing and focused concentration that helps to heal and maintain the physical body. The second word, *gong*, pronounced "gung," means accomplishment, or skill that is cultivated through steady practice. Qigong means cultivating energy. Qigong is a cornerstone of traditional Chinese medicine, and it has been practiced for thousands of years. It continues to be practiced today throughout Asia and is beginning to gain popularity throughout the world.

Qigong integrates physical postures, breathing techniques, and focused intentions. Although largely untapped for its healing here in the West, qigong is recognized by a growing number of medical studies for its wide-ranging benefits. (Centuries of empirical and anecdotal evidence speak to qigong's efficacy as a health care modality.) In the East, qigong has typically been indicated for a wide range of chronic illnesses, including, but not limited to:

1. Back or knee problems
2. Cardiovascular disease and other stress-related issues
3. Circulatory system disorders
4. Nervous system disorders
5. Addictions
6. Arthritis
7. Asthma
8. Mental illness

Besides countering the long-term effects of chronic stress/tension/pain and improving the function of the immune system, qigong's slow, gentle, and continuous movements produce many benefits including greater range of motion, reduced stress, increased stamina and vitality, improved muscle and soft tissue tone, and increased resilience.

The slow, deliberate, gentle movements of the qigong sequence allow the body and mind to relax, without dulling either. To the contrary, it improves consciousness and clarity, cultivates both attention and intention, and enhances self-awareness.

A set of exercises known as *PAL DAN GUM* is also referred to as the "eight silken movements." For thousands of years in China and Korea, sages have practiced these exercises for improving health, prolonging life, and aiding in spiritual development. Recommended for millennia by traditional Oriental doctors to cure diseases, modern hospitals continue their use today.

This short series of movements takes about five minutes and produces remarkable improvements in both mind and body. The movements immediately increase one's awareness and focus, along with more gradual improvements in flexibility, posture, circulation, and resiliency.

EXERCISE: PAL DAN GUM

Preparation: Begin by quietly walking around for a minute or two. Set your intention to quiet the mind and calm the body as you slowly and gently bring your attention to the breath. Lightly touch your tongue to your palate, as you concentrate on keeping the breath steady and regular, in and out through the nose.

As you move through the exercises, concentrate completely on the motions, postures, and breath. Allow your eyes to relax, keeping them soft and half opened. Flow smoothly from one exercise to the next, repeating any that you like. The entire series should take 5–10 minutes.

UPHOLDING HEAVEN (BOTH HANDS)

1. Stand in a stable way, with your feet apart, toes and eyes forward, and arms resting comfortably at your sides. Inhale slowly, bend your elbows as you bring your hands together just below the naval, interlock your fingers.

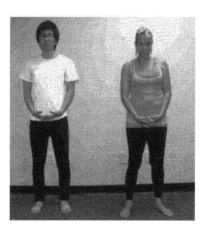

2. Now, turn your hands so that the palms are facing up. On the inhale, slowly raise your hands above your head, so that your hands are now together above your head, fingers interlocked, palms facing the floor.

3. Turn your hands so that your palms are now facing upward. Begin to push upward with the interlocked hands. As you do so, come up onto your toes, raising your heels slightly off the ground, and stretch toward the sky.

4. Maintain the pose for several seconds, continuing to stretch upward.

5. Exhale slowly, bringing your arms back to your sides as you come back down onto your heels.

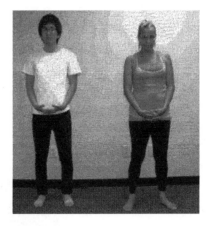

6. Return to the starting position.
7. Repeat this stretch twice.

STRETCHING THE BOW

1. Stand in a stable way, with your feet apart, toes forward, and your arms resting comfortably at your sides. Exhale as you step to the left with your left foot. Bend the knees and assume a horse-riding pose. Cross your arms in front of you at the wrists, left arm in front of the right. Clench both fists except for the left index finger, which should be extended.

2. As if you are holding a bow in your left hand and the bow string in your right, push the left arm out until it's straight out in front of you. Turn your head slowly to the left, while simultaneously pulling the right hand to the right chest, as if you are pulling the bow string. Focus your attention on the tip of the left index finger.

3. As you turn, inhale slowly. Hold the breath for several seconds, then exhale slowly through your nose as you allow your arms to relax at your side.

4. Inhale slowly. As you exhale, cross your arms in front of you, this time with the right arm in the front of the left, pointing the right index.

5. Open the bow once again, this time to the right side.

6. Inhale slowly. As you exhale, cross your arms in front of you, again with the left arm in front of the right, pointing the right index finger.

7. Repeat sequence twice.

UPHOLDING HEAVEN AND EARTH

1. Stand in a stable way, with your feet apart, toes forward, and your arms resting comfortably at your sides.

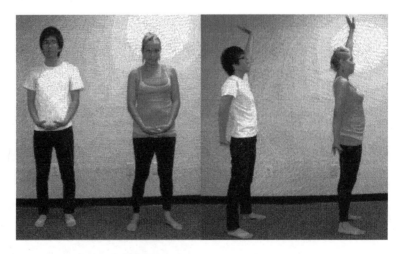

2. Raise your hands to the level of the navel, keeping your palms facing up and your elbows straight to the sides. The fingertips will slightly touch.

3. Raise your left hand above your head, rotating the arm so that that palm faces upward (with fingers pointed inward). Simultaneously, lower your right hand, palm facing down, and fingers pointed inward, to your right side. Stretch both arms.

4. Return to the starting position.

5. Repeat the exercise on the other side.

6. Repeat both sequences twice.

LOOKING BACKWARDS

1. Stand in a stable way, with your feet apart, toes forward, and your arms resting comfortably at your sides.

2. Cross your hands several inches in front of your face, with your right hand closer to your face.. Now, pull your hands to your sides and back, straightening your arms and turning your palms forward. Without rotating at the waist, gently and slowly turn your head to the left as far as it will comfortably go.

3. Return to the starting position.

4. Again, cross your hands in front of you, but this time with your left hand closer to your face. Pull your hands to your sides and back, straightening your arms and turning your palms forward. Without rotating at the waist, gently and slowly turn your head to the right as far as it will comfortably go.

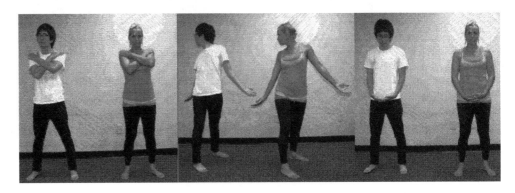

5. Repeat sequence twice.

BENDING SIDEWAYS

1. Stand in a stable way, with your feet apart, toes forward, and your arms resting comfortably at your sides. Spread your legs, as if assuming a horse-riding pose, and place your hands on your hips.

2. Bend your body to the left side. Allow your shoulders and head to tilt to the left. Breathe into the stretch.

3. Return to the starting position.

4. Bend your body and head to the right side. Allow your shoulders and head to tilt to the right. Breathe into the stretch.

5. Return again to the starting position.

6. Bend your body and head forward. Allow your head to hang freely, as you breathe into the stretch. Bend backwards as far as you comfortably can. Breathe into the stretch.

7. Return to the starting position.

8. Slowly and gently tilt your head to the right. Breathe into the stretch. Slowly and gently tilt your head to the left. Breathe into the stretch.

9. Slowly and gently tilt your head forward. Breathe into the stretch. Slowly and gently tilt your head backwards. Breathe into the stretch.

10. Return to the starting position. Relax your neck completely and slowly rotate your head, first counterclockwise and then clockwise.

11. Return to the starting position.
12. Repeat the sequence twice.

PUNCHING WITH ANGRY EYES

1. Stand in a stable way, with your feet apart, toes forward, and your arms resting comfortably at your sides. Step to the left and bend your knees to assume the horse-riding pose.

2. Place your fists, palms up, shoulder high, elbows at your side. Open your eyes very wide.

3. With the left fist, punch to the left, watching your knuckles throughout. Return your left arm to its previous position.

4. With the right fist, punch to the right, watching your knuckles throughout.

5. Return your right arm to its previous position. Punch forward with your left fist and return.

6. Punch forward with your right fist.

7. Return to the starting position.
8. Punch to the left side with the left fist and return.

9. Punch to the right side with the right fist.

10. Return to the starting position.

11. Repeat the sequence twice.

STANDING ON TOES

1. Stand in a stable way, with your feet apart, toes forward, and your arms resting comfortably at your sides.

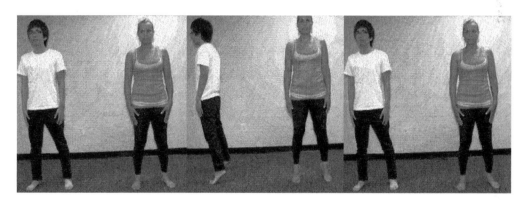

2. Raise your heels slowly and hold the extended position for several seconds.

3. Slowly return the heels to the ground.

4. Repeat two more times

BENDING OVER AND STRETCHING THE BACK

1. Stand in a stable way, with your feet apart, toes forward and your hands on your hips.

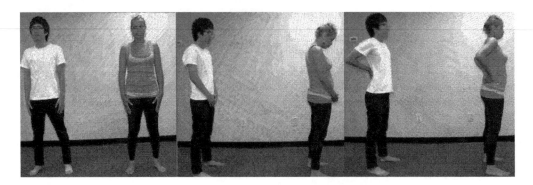

2. Interlace the fingers of both hands, inhale and raise them over your head.

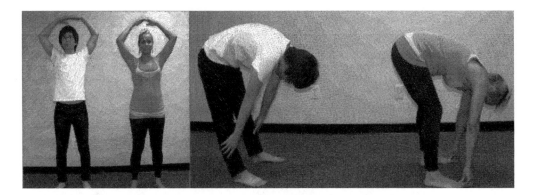

3. On the exhale, gently lean your body forward, keeping your knees straight. Allow your body to hang down. Breathe as you allow gravity to stretch your back.

4. Come back up slowly and gently returning to the starting position with your hands on the back of your hips.

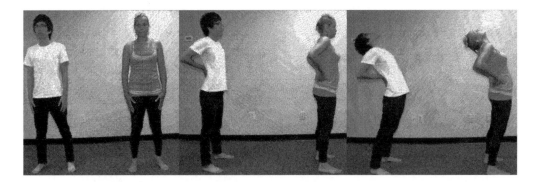

5. Slowly and gently arch your head back as you look backward.

6. Come back up slowly and gently, returning to the starting position, with your hands by your sides.

7. Repeat twice more.

Body Language

Our expression and our words never coincide, which is why the animals don't understand us.

~Malcolm de Chazal

David McNeill at the University of Chicago describes body gestures as our "windows into thought processes." Gestures, facial expressions, and body postures are social signals, ways of communicating our intentions and our feelings with one another. Fortunately (or unfortunately), whether consciously or unconsciously, our bodies are almost always conveying something about us to other people, and vice versa.

MIRRORING

When people are free to do as they please, they usually imitate each other.

~Eric Hoffer

Mirroring, a process akin to active witnessing, provides a means of raising awareness and gathering data. Mirror neurons are the only brain cells we know of that seem specialized to code our own actions and the actions of other people. They are obviously essential for social interactions. Without them, we would likely be blind to the actions, intentions, and emotions of other people.

Marco Iacoboni, a neuroscientist at the University of California, San Diego, is one of several mirror neuron researchers who have proposed a simple mechanism for explaining empathy through the actions of mirror neurons. He states that when we *see* an emotion-laden action, our mirror neuron systems *automatically simulate* what is happening in the motor centers of the other person's brain (without causing us to execute any action). He posits that this brain simulation process produces the same sensations that accompany the bodily actions of the other person. For example, when we see somebody smile, we often respond by smiling back, but even if we don't, we *know* that (s)he is smiling in happiness. Although we can consciously imagine what somebody else is feeling, our mirror neuron system provides a more direct link from another person's emotional state to our own. We feel what the other person feels, weakly, perhaps, but immediately, automatically, without conscious reflection. The most basic function of the mirror neuron system is to help us understand what's happening inside other people's heads by observing external cues, both their own actions and various other facets of the situation. We automatically take this intuitive knowledge into account when we navigate social situations.

In his book, *Mirroring People: The Science of Empathy and How We Connect with Others,* Iacoboni (2008) explains mirroring and mirror neurons:

> "Mirror neurons are the cells in our brains that make our experience, mostly made of interactions with other people, deeply meaningful. ...

Mirror neurons are brain cells that seem specialized in understanding our existential condition and our involvement with others. They show that we are not alone, but are biologically wired and evolutionarily designed to be deeply interconnected with one another. (p. 267)

Kierkegaard proposed that our existence becomes meaningful only through our authentic commitment to the finite and temporal, a commitment that defines us. The neural resonance between self and other that mirror neurons allow is, in my opinion, the embodiment of such commitment. Our neurobiology—our mirror neurons—commits us to others. Mirror neurons show the deepest way we relate to and understand each other: they demonstrate that *we are wired for empathy*, which should inspire us to shape our society and make it a better place to live. (p. 268)

Consciously or unconsciously, our bodies are communicating with other bodies. It's probably a worthy endeavor to be informed of exactly **what** it is that we are communicating.

Mirroring Exercises

GROUP

INSTRUCTIONS:

This is a completely nonverbal exercise.

The facilitator should offer a demonstration. Invite a volunteer to stand facing you about two feet apart. The facilitator initiates action, with the other person following in "mirror image." The facilitator should make the movements interesting and slow enough for the other person to mime as if they were a full-length mirror.

Invite participants to pair off and either sit or stand together. Once in pairs, one person in each dyad is invited to take the role of leader.

Once decided, the leader is instructed to begin to move in any way that (s)he wishes, while the other participant is instructed to follow or mimic every behavior—both obvious and subtle—that the leader displays.

Allow this to go on for a minute or two, then instruct the pair to switch roles. Instruct the new leader to begin to move in any way that (s)he wishes, while the other participant follows, mimicking every behavior—both obvious and subtle—that the leader displays.

Allow this to go on for a minute or two, then instruct the pair to do the exercise one last time, but this time neither participant is the leader or the follower. Instruct both participants to try to move in unison, as if they are mirroring each other simultaneously in a *dance of body language*.

This "dance" is somewhat hard to do and takes a bit of practice before a pair gets the hang of it, if they can do it at all. If the pair IS successful, what usually happens is rapid, minute shifts between leading and following.

Have participants switch partners several times and repeat the preceding steps.

- Further experiments involve the mirroring with body language alone, facial expressions alone, or body language with facial expressions.
- Processing of the exercises should include questions such as the following:
  1. How sensitive or empathically in tune was each participant to the details of the partner's body movements and expressions?
  2. What information was gathered regarding participants' interpersonal styles? For example, was there a strong preference to "lead" versus "follow"?
  3. At what level were the participants able to move in unison? For example, how "in sync" was each dyad? What accounts for that?
  4. Was it markedly easier with some people and more difficult with others?
  5. What, if any, generalizations can be made from this mirroring exercise?

Regulating the Dysregulated Autonomic Nervous System

AUTONOMIC NERVOUS SYSTEM

The body's autonomic nervous system (ANS) governs many of the body's internal functions, through its two branches: the *sympathetic branch (SNS)* ("fight-or-flight") of this ANS activates or increases the heart's action, while the *parasympathetic branch (PNS)* ("rest" and "digest") acts as a brake slowing the action of the heart. The vagus nerve plays a role in parasympathetic braking action. (See **The Polyvagal Theory**, which follows.) The balance between this acceleration and braking system produces an ongoing oscillation, a systematic increase and decrease in heart rate.

These autonomic inputs are mediated by two "pacemakers" in the heart; the sinoatrial (SA) and atrioventricular (AV) nodes, which are responsible for heart rhythms. The SA node initiates an electrical signal that begins each cycle of the heart's pumping action. This signal passes through the AV node, which spreads the electrical current through the ventricles of the heart. A variety of factors, including breathing, pressure sensors (baroreceptors) in the arteries, the body's thermal regulation, and anxious thinking, increase specific rhythms in heart activity. The overall process of heart function is the end product of these component rhythms.

HEART RATE VARIABILITY (HRV)

Unlike a clock that ticks continuously at a steady, unchanging rate, the human heart is a bio-electrical pump that beats at an ever changing rate. **HRV** is the change in the interval or distance between one beat of the heart and the next. Measured in milliseconds, this *interbeat interval* (**IBI**) is the duration between one heart beat and the next. The **IBI** is highly variable within any given time period. Multiple biological rhythms overlay each other to produce the resultant pattern of variability. **IBI** variations, or *heart rate variability*, have relevance for physical, emotional, and mental function.

> **HRV is a measurement: High is good; Low is poor.**
> **High HRV has been associated with heart health, while low HRV**
> **has been associated with illness.**

Clinical findings confirm the importance of the high **HRV**; it is an especially adaptive quality for the maintenance of a healthy body. Studies have also shown that chronically traumatized people have significantly low **HRV**. *Luckily, high or low HRV is not necessarily a permanent condition, because the autonomic nervous system can be changed.* The following exercises are designed to trigger the PNS (the part of your nervous system that creates positive feeling, thereby reducing stress, enhancing positive emotion, and ultimately strengthening the body's immune system). By intentionally and purposefully activating the parasympathetic branch of your nervous system, you can curb the cycle of chronic stress.

THE POLYVAGAL THEORY

The polyvagal theory proposes that the evolution of the mammalian autonomic nervous system provides the neurophysiological substrates for adaptive behavioral strategies. It further proposes that physiological state limits the range of behavior and psychological experience. The theory links the evolution of the autonomic nervous system to affective experience, emotional expression, facial gestures, vocal communication, and contingent social behavior. *In this way, the theory provides a plausible explanation for the reported covariation between atypical autonomic regulation (e.g., reduced vagal and increased sympathetic influences to the heart) and psychiatric and behavioral disorders that involve difficulties in regulating appropriate social, emotional, and communication behaviors.*

The polyvagal theory provides several insights into the adaptive nature of physiological states. First, the theory emphasizes that physiological states support different classes of behavior. For example, a physiological state characterized by a vagal withdrawal would support the mobilization behaviors of fight and flight. In contrast, a physiological state characterized by increased vagal influence on the heart (via myelinated vagal pathways originating in the nucleus ambiguus) would support spontaneous social engagement behaviors. Second, the theory emphasizes the formation of an integrated social engagement system through functional and structural links between neural control of the striated muscles of the face and the smooth muscles of the viscera. Third, the polyvagal theory proposes a mechanism—neuroception—to trigger or to inhibit defense strategies. (p. 90)

Excerpted with permission from Stephen Porges, Ph.D., Porges SW. (2009). *The polyvagal theory: New insights into adaptive reactions of the autonomic nervous system.* Cleveland Clinic Journal of Medicine, 76:S86-90..

RECOMMENDATION:

If you are unfamiliar with the polyvagal theory, it means that you have not yet read Porges's new book, *The Polyvagal Theory: Neurophysiological Foundations of Emotions, Attachment, Communication, and Self-regulation.* I highly recommend that you rectify this situation; get it, read it, read it again, and then incorporate it into your clinical practice. You will thank me.

Regulating the Dysregulated Autonomic Nervous System

EXERCISES FOR ACTIVATING THE PNS

YAWNING

Here's an extremely contagious method for activating the PNS: yawning. If you haven't voluntarily or involuntarily initiated a yawn yet, it's a safe bet that you will while reading the next few sentences.

Yawning is a natural respiratory reflex that improves circulation to the face, relaxes the eyes, and counteracts the shallow, rapid breathing that is generally associated with stress. Yawning requires a deep, slow inhalation, followed by a full exhalation. Because yawning triggers the relaxation response, you should repeat it as often as you like; it's cheap, portable, and effective.

INSTRUCTIONS (JUST IN CASE YOU'VE FORGOTTEN):

1. Sit or stand comfortably.
2. Shrug, rotate, then shake out your shoulders for a few seconds.
3. Locate your jaw joints by putting your fingers on both jaws. Add a slight bit of pressure as you begin to open and close your mouth, as you feel the joints with your fingertips.
4. Once you've located the joints, begin to lightly massage those muscles. (The jaw muscles can exert the strongest force; consequently they tend to be the most tense muscles in the body.)
5. As you continue to massage any tight spots, begin to open your mouth, and slowly begin to inhale.
6. Open your mouth a bit wider . . . wider . . . wider.
7. Open the back of your throat. Allow the air to rush through your breathing passages.
8. At the end of the inhalation, complete the yawn by exhaling loudly with a "huff" or a sigh.
9. Allow your breath to return to normal.
10. Take a few deeper breaths.

11. Remain sitting or standing comfortably.

12. This time, in addition to stretching your face muscles as you begin the open-mouthed inhale, without straining, stretch your arms out wide to the sides, then stretch them up as far up as comfortably possible.

13. Pay attention to the muscles as they stretch.

14. After you have deeply inhaled and fully stretched, complete the yawn by exhaling loudly with a "huff" or a sigh, while dropping your arms to your sides.

THE MAMMALIAN DIVING REFLEX

As far as we know, every mammal has an automated response system for diving in cold water (less than about 21°C). This mammalian diving reflex allows dive times to be extended by maximizing oxygen expenditure efficiency while submerged.

Briefly, this reflex allows the body to enter a state of hibernation in which oxygen depletion is less detrimental to the brain, which increases the odds of survival in cold water drownings.

The following parasympathetic nervous system responses are typical (and in this order):

1. The heart rate slows.
2. The blood flow to extremities becomes constricted.
3. The blood and water are allowed to pass through organs and circulatory walls into chest cavity.

The first two items begin to happen immediately (i.e., as soon as the face hits cold water). The slowing heart rate is almost instantaneous, while the constricted blood flow happens more gradually.

1. The slowed heart rate serves to conserve oxygen (preventing depletion), thereby increasing the amount of available time underwater without dramatically impairing performance.

2. The decreased blood flow provides more of a long-term (minutes to hours) survival benefit, but seriously impairs performance.

3. The third response is a bit more scary, because the body *intentionally allows fluid to fill the lungs and chest cavity* (to prevent organs from being crushed from extreme pressure). For surface-dwelling mammals, it serves a survival function and therefore only kicks in as depths become extreme.

Interesting. But what does it have to do with trauma-informed interventions?

Well, when one is in a state of extreme emotional arousal, information processing suffers dramatically. In order to recover this crucial function, the nervous system essentially needs to be reset or rebooted. Marsha Linehan, Ph.D. (of DBT fame) and others have posited that the activation of the mammalian diving reflex is an effective method of doing just that. The reflex can be voluntarily activated by submerging one's head in a bowl of ice water (not freezing) or splashing one's face (just below the eyes and above the cheekbones) with icy cold water.

INSTRUCTIONS:

- Fill a bowl with icy cold water.
- Bend/lean over.
- Hold your breath.
- Put face in icy cold water for 30 seconds.
- Make sure that most sensitive part of the face (area underneath eyes/above cheekbones) feels the icy water.

Linehan claims (and this author concurs) that this surprisingly simple technique is "incredibly effective in calming down immediately."

Additional methods for activating the diving reflex include placing an ice cold gel pack or mask over/around the eye area or holding one's breath for 30 seconds while bending forward.

WHO SHOULDN'T DO THIS:

- Anyone with bradycardia (heart rate < 60 beats per minute)
- Anyone with known cardiac problems
- Anyone with an eating disorder (particularly anorexia nervosa)

HAND WARMING

When we are stressed, blood is shunted away from our hands and feet and directed to vital organs and the large muscles of our shoulders, hips, and thighs, enabling us to react physically to danger (i.e., fight or flee). But as you well know, most times the stress response is inappropriate for present situation (i.e., we are not in grave danger—being neither chased nor attacked).

The more stressed a person is, the lower the temperature in the hands; the lower the stress level, the higher the temperature should be in the hands. (Research has shown that stress causes at least one or two degree Fahrenheit decrease over a five-minute period.)

A biofeedback technique, aptly named, *hand warming*, is designed to counteract the stress response via increasing parasympathetic activation. By simultaneously focusing your attention on your hands, while mentally conjuring images of warmth (e.g., holding a cup of hot chocolate, sitting by a fireplace, caressing someone's warm skin, or sitting in a sauna or hot tub) you can actually increase the temperature of your hands, consequently inducing a general sense of calm in your body and mind.

Learning to warm your hands via your thoughts requires no biofeedback instruments, just a little bit of relaxation training. However, in order to measure and track changes in temperature, you may wish to get a monitor. Alternatively, a much cheaper option would be to get a *stress card*.

Stress Check Magic Word biosquare cards provide an inexpensive tool for thermal biofeedback-aided relaxation and stress management training. (To order, go to: www.futurehealth.org.)

INSTRUCTIONS: GUIDED IMAGERY SCRIPT FOR *HAND WARMING*

Allow yourself to be comfortable . . . either lying down or sitting up with your back, neck, and spine fully supported. Knowing that you will not be interrupted for the next little while, begin by gently closing your eyes.

Now begin to bring your attention to your breath—the direct experience of your breath—however it is . . . and however it changes. Allow yourself to softly focus your awareness onto the breath that is arising right now. . . the in-breath and the out-breath . . . the rising and the falling. If you can, try to follow one full cycle of the breath from the beginning of the in-breath and through its entirety to the beginning of the out-breath and through its entirety. Allow yourself the time and the space to be in direct contact with the breath throughout one entire cycle.

As you continue to pay attention to the breath, gently guide your awareness to your hands, noticing any sensations, energy, and the temperature in your hands. Bring to mind an image of warmth. Perhaps you are sitting by a fire, or warm and cozy under some blankets, possibly cuddled up with a loved one or pet, or lying on the beach under the blazing sun. Whatever brings with it the sense of warmth . . . heat.

Once you have the image, allow it to become as vivid as possible.

Now, feeling the warmth, begin to notice your breath again . . . coming slowly and easily. Deepening with each inhalation . . . exhale fully and completely. Feel the warmth on your skin . . . completely comfortable . . . completely relaxed.

As the next breath arises, pay attention to this deep and comforting relaxation. Breathe here for a moment. . . .

And when you are ready, gently bring yourself back to this room by counting up from one to five. When you reach the number five, your eyes will gently open. You will be awake and alert, feeling only peace. One . . . two . . . three. Take a deep breath . . . four . . . and five.

BONUS

We already know that breathing rate affects heart rate patterns, which, in turn, affects how the brain deals with stress. We also know that it is difficult to directly control one's own heart rate or brain function. However, one can fairly easily control his/her breathing rate. It turns out that by regularly (voluntarily) slowing one's breathing down, one can improve *heart rate variability,* thereby allowing the brain to effectively deal with the stressful situations you encounter.

MyCalmBeat is a brain exercise by MyBrainSolutions that helps improve your ability to manage stress through slow breathing. Slow breathing allows you to increase the variability of your heart rate to decrease stress, improve focus, and build resilience.

MyCalmBeat works by increasing your heart rate variability through slow breathing. It first calculates your personal best breathing rate (when you are most calm) and then gives you tools to train by breathing at that rate. *MyCalmBeat* is a free app for your computer and/or smart phone. It is available from www.mybrainsolutions.com/mycalmbeat.

Holding Neurovascular Points

Neurovascular points are specific spots on the head that activate blood flow to the area. The area of interest is the prefrontal cortex—the part of the brain responsible for, among other things, regulating the amygdala's response to stress, planning, decision making, and executive function.

Holding the neurovascular points while thinking about a stressor seems to suspend the stress response by preventing the blood from leaving the forebrain, in other words, keeping the prefrontal cortex engaged in top-down regulation of the amygdala. By interrupting a key component of the fight-or-flight response, the *neurovascular hold* allows us to think more clearly while contending with difficulties.

INSTRUCTIONS:

1. Locate the two points with your fingertips. They are midway between your hairline and your eyebrows, directly over the midpoint of each eyebrow.

2. Using the fingertips of both hands, apply light pressure while stretching the skin taut, eliminating any slack.

3. Continue holding the pressure as you inhale to the count of four. Pause. Exhale to the count of four.

4. Bring to mind a stressful situation—past, present, or future.

5. Keeping the stressor in mind, continue holding the pressure as you inhale again to the count of four. Pause. Exhale to the count of five.

6. Continue holding the pressure as you inhale again to the count of four. Pause. Exhale to the count of six.

7. Continue holding the pressure as you inhale again to the count of four. Pause. Exhale to the count of seven.

8. Continue holding the pressure as you inhale again to the count of four. Pause. Exhale to the count of eight.

9. Repeat often.

Acupressure Points

HOLDING, THUMPING, AND TAPPING

Both Western and Eastern medicine agree that there is a need to keep the electromagnetic circuits of the body (described as meridians in the Chinese system of acupuncture) flowing freely. During periods of increased stress, levels of both adrenalin and cortisol rise, consequently lowering the electrical potential across neuronal membranes in preparation for the short-term defensive actions of fight or flight. In this survival state, the body directs electrical energy away from the neocortex (thinking part of the brain) and toward subcortical area—specifically, the sympathetic branch of the autonomic system. In an actual emergency, this response is adaptive and life-saving; however, oftentimes in traumatized people, no danger is actually **present**, just a reminder of a past trauma. That reminder keeps inappropriately alerting the brain and body to continue dumping the stress hormones into the bloodstream.

The following exercises are designed to counter the *misguided* activation of the sympathetic nervous system, by stimulating the parasympathetic function of the autonomic nervous system. This stimulation decreases the release of adrenalin and cortisol and increases the electrical potential across neuronal membrane, thus allowing the prefrontal cortex (i.e., the thinking part of the brain) to reengage. In addition to the decrease in stress hormones, the semicircular canals of the inner ear are also stimulated by the electrical activity that occurs during the movements. These canals activate a part of the brainstem called the reticular formation (whose job it is to screen out distracting stimuli), which in turn creates a more awake, alert, and focused attention in the thinking part of the brain.

HOLDING K-27 POINTS

The purpose of holding these points is to activate certain brain areas to:

- Improve communication between the right brain hemisphere and the left side of the body, and vice versa.
- Increase blood supply to the brain.
- Increase in oxygen intake.
- Increase flow of electromagnetic energy.

The K-27 points are located just below the collarbone. To find them, place your fingertips on the U-shaped notch at the top of the sternum. Move your fingers down one inch, then out toward each shoulder.

INSTRUCTIONS:

1. First locate the K-27 points and massage both sides.
2. Now, spread the fingers on your right hand and place it with the palm side down over your breastbone and heart (covering both K-27 points)

3. Now, spread the fingers on your left hand and place it with the palm side down over your navel.

4. With a bit of pressure, begin to hold these points.

5. Continue holding the pressure, as you inhale to the count of four. Pause. Exhale to the count of four.

6. Continue holding the pressure, as you inhale to the count of four. Pause. Exhale to the count of five.

7. Continue holding the pressure, as you inhale again to the count of four. Pause. Exhale to the count of six.

8. Continue holding the pressure, as you inhale again to the count of four. Pause. Exhale to the count of seven.

9. Continue holding the pressure, as you inhale again to the count of four. Pause. Exhale to the count of eight.

10. Repeat often.

THREE THUMPS

(Adapted from Donna Eden's *Energy Medicine Five-Minute Daily Routine*.)

thump: *(verb)*

    to hit heavily

    do something with a heavy deadened sound

    (noun) a heavy dull blow

This exercise is the only instance in the entire book in which you will not be asked to be gentle with yourself, because the next series of exercises only work if you vigorously thump the acupressure points. (Obvious contraindications, such as injuries to the area, medical implants, etc., apply.)

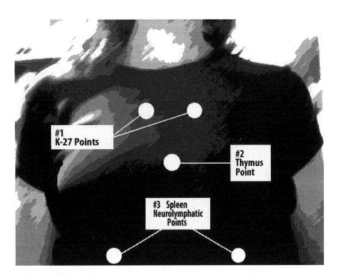

(1) **Thump K-27:** The K-27 points are located just below the collarbone. To find them, place your fingertips on the U-shaped notch at the top of the sternum.

INSTRUCTIONS:

1. Move your fingers down one inch, then out toward each shoulder.
2. Bring your fingers together as shown.

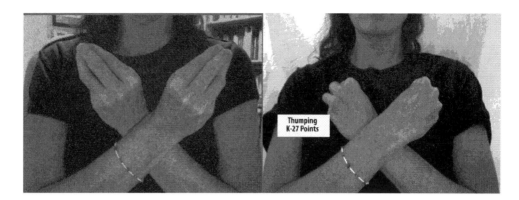

3. Cross your hands so that the left hand thumps the right point and the right hand thumps the left point.
4. Breathing deeply in and out through your nose, begin thumping the K-27 points.
5. After three deep breaths, allow your arms to return to your sides and relax.

(2) **Thump the Thymus Gland:** The thymus gland, which plays a vital role in the body's immune system, is located in the center of the chest, on the upper part of the sternum, just between your nipples. For this thumping, you will choose an affirmation from the following list, or if none of those fit, conjure your own. You will repeat it to yourself (silently or aloud), as you vigorously thump the thymus gland. The key to benefiting from affirmations is to feel the feelings depicted in the words you are saying; so pick one that works for you.

I am calm.
I am peaceful.
I am loved.
I am centered.
I choose to see the good in the people.
I will make time to breathe.
I can control my reactions to today's challenges.
I have been blessed over and over again.
I live my life with gratitude.
I am whole and perfect just as I am
I give thanks continually as I move through each day.
I can make a difference.

INSTRUCTIONS:

1. Once you've settled on an affirmation, begin by breathing deeply in and out through your nose.
2. Bring your fingers together as shown, and begin thumping the point in the center of the chest, as you speak you affirmation.

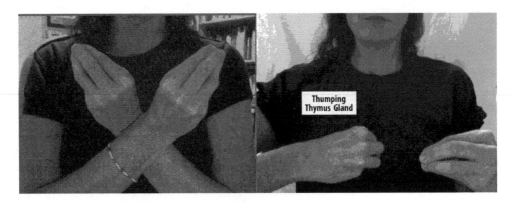

3. After three deep breaths, allow your arms to return to your sides and relax.

(3) Thump the Spleen Neurolymphatic Points

The spleen neurolymphatic points are the depression between the seventh and eighth ribs, just below the level of the sternum. To locate these points, begin at about three or four inches under your armpit and continue along this line (the bra line if you are a woman) to the point directly under the nipples.

*The spleen neurolymphatic points are generally sore, so you may want to begin by rubbing them, and as the soreness diminishes, switch over to thumping.

INSTRUCTIONS:

1. Begin by breathing deeply in and out through your nose.
2. Bring your fingers together as shown.
3. Breathing deeply in and out through your nose, begin thumping the neurolymphatic points.
4. After three deep breaths, allow your arms to return to your sides and relax.

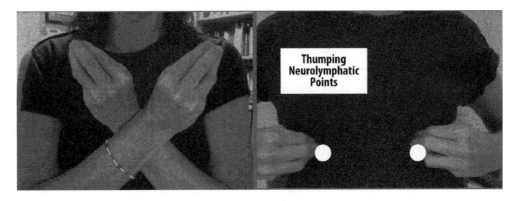

Emotional Freedom Technique (EFT)

EFT has been described a needle-less acupuncture for the emotions. Along with the simpler, all-purpose tapping protocol, EFT also instructs people to speak affirmations and engage in unusual, yet seemingly effective behaviors, including tapping, eye movements, humming, and counting. Gary Craig, a student of Roger Callahan, developed EFT, by combining the eye movements and emphasis on shifting underlying cognitive belief systems of Eye Movement Desensitization and Reprogramming (EMDR) with a more generalized acupressure point tapping, based on TFT. One cycle of EFT takes only a few minutes, generates little distress, and can be effective even if the client does not believe that it will be. No formal research studies have been done to empirically prove the efficacy of these acupressure techniques. However, clinicians and clients alike seem impressed with the results that they've been getting (author included).

According to van der Kolk and colleagues (1996), effective treatment requires exposure to, without total reexperiencing of, the traumatic material; too much arousal precludes assimilation of any new information. It may be that the tapping protocol in TFT and EFT provides a concrete physical stimulus drawing attention back to the here and now, anchoring clients in the present. It also appears that the physical, rhythmic stimulation has a calming and soothing effect on agitated clients. This calming is most likely produced by the reciprocal inhibitory relaxation response of the parasympathetic nervous system as it reduces the effects of the hyperactivated sympathetic nervous system (Carbonell and Figley, 1995). In EFT, you tap gently on certain acupuncture meridians on the face and the body as you tune into the problem you want to resolve. The tapping process, combined with your focused attention on the issue you want to resolve, can reduce physical and emotional pains, end cravings/habits, and relieve anxiety, fears, and phobias, sometimes with remarkable speed and often with long-lasting positive effects.

The EFT "Basic Recipe"

Usually one can learn the basic recipe within a few minutes. Once familiar with this process, you can do the whole round in less than two minutes.

To begin: Identify the specific problem and observe how it feels: thoughts, sensations, and emotions that are associated with the issue. Using a subjective units of distress scale (SUDS), rate your distress from 0 to 10 (0 = no distress, 10 = the worst distress you can imagine).

Follow the four components of the "Basic Recipe."

1. THE SETUP

- Start your EFT process by tapping firmly on your karate chop point.
- Set up phrase: Next, bring up the negative emotion and/or problem you want to address.
- Note the SUDS level from 0 to 10 (0 = none, 10 = worst).
- Then say the following statement three times and with some degree of conviction (aloud if possible, though not necessary) as you firmly tap on the karate chop point: "Even though I have this _____, I accept myself." (Fill the blank with the negative emotion or issue you want to address.) For example: "Even though I have this craving for chocolate, I completely accept myself" or "Even though I feel so angry at him, I completely accept myself."

2. THE SEQUENCE

- Once the setup step is complete, place your index finger and middle finger together.
- Using the tips of these fingers, tap about seven times on each of the meridian points listed.
- Tap firmly—but not so hard that you bruise or hurt yourself. (Most of the tapping points exist on both sides of the body. It doesn't matter whether you tap on the right side or the left, nor does it matter if you switch sides during the sequence. For example, you can tap under your right eye and, later in the sequence, tap under your left eye.)
- As you tap on these points, it is necessary to keep your mind tuned to the issue you are resolving with EFT.
- To do that, say a reminder phrase: "This _____ (issue) . . ." as you tap on each of the points.
- Using the example of chocolate craving, the reminder phrase would be, "This craving for chocolate."
- Going down the face and the body, gently tap on the following points as you say your reminder phrase, "This _____ (issue)," starting from:

MERIDIAN TAPPING POINTS

1. Sore Spot = Find the U-shaped notch at the top of your sternum and from the top of that notch go down 3 inches toward your navel and over 3 inches toward your shoulder.

2. Karate Chop = Soft fleshy part of the nondominant hand, between the base of the pinky finger and the wrist.

3. EB = Beginning of the eyebrow (either the left or right one).

4. SE = Side of your eye (of either left or right eye, tap on the bony part of the eye socket right at the corner of your eye. Don't get so close to the eye that you hurt yourself, but don't go so far off that you are tapping on your temple.).

5. UE = Under the eye (of either the left or right eye, again on the bony part of the eye socket, about 1 inch below the pupil).

6. UN = Under the nose (and the top of the lip).

7. CH = Chin (midway between the chin and the bottom of lower lip).

8. CB = Beginning of the collarbone (where the breastbone, collarbone, and first rib meet).

9. UA = Under the arm (about 4 inches below your armpit on either side).

10. TH = Top of the head.

3. THE 9 GAMUT PROCEDURES

After completing the sequence, you are now ready to carry out "The 9-Gamut Procedure." This procedure fine-tunes the brain via eye movements, humming, and counting so as to enhance the effects of the tapping. It tunes the brain to the right frequency for the problem. Through connecting nerves, certain parts of the brain are stimulated when eyes are moved. Likewise, the right side of the brain is engaged when you hum a song and the left side is engaged when you count. During this procedure, nine of these brain-stimulating actions are performed while simultaneously and continuously tapping the gamut point. While continually tapping on the gamut point, carry out all the following:

BRAIN-BALANCING STEPS

1. Close your eyes.

2. Open your eyes.

3. Eyes hard down right while holding the head steady (stimulates kinesthetic sensations and memory).

4. Eyes hard down left while holding the head steady (internal dialogue).

5. Roll the eyes in a circle clockwise (stimulates visual and auditory memory and imagination).

6. Roll the eyes counter-clockwise.

7. Hum "Happy Birthday," or any song, for two bars (this engages the right brain).

8. Count to 5 (this engages the left brain).

9. Hum "Happy Birthday," or any song, for two bars again (this engages the right brain).

4. THE SEQUENCE (ONCE AGAIN):

After completing the 9-Gamut procedure, repeat the whole sequence: take a deep breath, check in, and reassess.

- After each round of EFT, take a deep breath in and gently breathe out.
- Take a moment to check in with yourself.
- Notice how you are feeling now, physically and emotionally; notice what thoughts, memories, or emotions are up for you.
- Without judging yourself right or wrong, just observe.
- Next, reassess the intensity level of the problem.
- What is the intensity level now? If you are at a 0, you are done. Congratulations!
- If not, you may need to do one or more subsequent rounds until you feel the intensity has gone down to 0.

MERIDIAN TAPPING POINTS

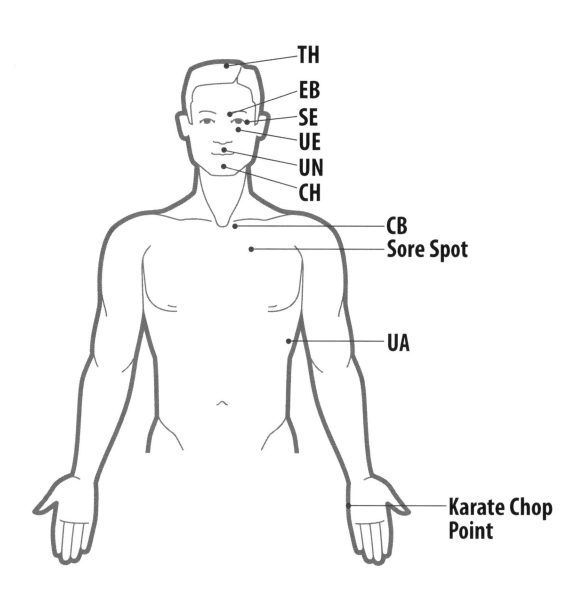

TH
EB
SE
UE
UN
CH
CB
Sore Spot
UA
Karate Chop Point

Improving Right/Left Hemispheric Communication

(Variations on these exercises can be found on various websites, such as http://www.innersource. net/ep/ and www.learnenergymedicine.com under various labels.)

These exercises assist in reestablishing neural connections between the body and brain, thus facilitating the flow of electromagnetic energy throughout the body: (1) left-to-right/right-to-left, (2) top-to-bottom/bottom-to-top, and (3) back-to-front/front-to-back circuits. All of which serve to establish and support one's sense of direction and provide a more centered focus and greater awareness of proprioception (awareness of where one is in space and in relation to objects in the environment).

"When energy is unable to cross over, it slows down dramatically. It begins to move in a homolateral pattern straight up and down the body and the body's ability to heal is severely diminished."

~Donna Eden & David Feinstein, Ph.D.

CROSS CRAWL

(Adapted from Donna Eden's *Energy Medicine: Five-Minute Daily Routine*)

The cross crawl exercise accesses both brain hemispheres, simultaneously stimulating the receptive (left) as well as the expressive (right) hemisphere of the brain, thereby facilitating communication and integration.

INSTRUCTIONS:

In this contralateral exercise, similar to marching in place, the participant alternately moves one arm and its opposite leg and then the other arm and its opposite leg.

Using Sound, Music, and Vocalizations to Regulate the Autonomic Nervous System

Song Sung Blue

~Neil Diamond

Song sung blue

Weeping like a willow

Song sung blue

Sleeping on my pillow

Funny thing, but you can sing it with a cry in your voice

And before you know it, get to feeling good

You simply got no choice

CLINICAL APPLICATION:

"**How music and prosodic vocalizations can trigger the Social Engagement System.** ...Vocal music duplicates the effect of vocal prosody and triggers neural mechanisms that regulate the entire Social Engagement System with the resultant changes in facial affect and autonomic state. *Basically, we start to look and feel better when we listen to melodies.*

". . . Based on the Polyvagal Theory we are able to deconstruct music therapy into biobehavioral processes that stimulate the Social Engagement System. When the system is stimulated, the client responds both behaviorally and physiologically. First, the observable features of social engagement become more spontaneous and contingent. The face and voice become more expressive. Second, there is a change in physiological state regulation that is expressed in more regulated and calmer behavior. The improved state regulation is mediated by the myelinated vagus nerve, which directly promotes health, growth, and restoration. However for some clients, especially those who have been traumatized, face-to-face interactions are threatening and do not elicit a *neuroception* of safety. If this is the case, then the Social Engagement System can potentially be triggered through vocal prosody or music while minimizing direct face-to-face interactions.

". . . Music, and especially vocal music, produces melodies by modulating these frequencies. This process engages and exercises the neural regulation of the Social Engagement System with the positive effects of improved socio-emotional behaviors and enhanced physiological state. Interestingly, the phrasing of music is also an important component of this process. The phrasing of music, especially when singing or playing a wind instrument, results in short inhalations and extended durations of exhalations. Physiologically, breathing 'gates' the influence of the myelinated vagus nerve on the heart. Functionally, when we inhale, the influence of the vagus is attenuated and heart rate increases. In contrast, when we exhale, the influence of the vagus is increased and heart rate decreases. This simple mechanical change in breathing increases the calming impact and health benefits of the myelinated vagus on our body. Thus, music therapy by engaging and exercising the Social Engagement System may promote positive outcomes improving several features related to quality of life." (Excerpted with permission from S.W. Porges, "Music Therapy and Trauma," 2010)

Finding Your Voice: Expanding the Throat

INDIVIDUAL OR GROUP

Most of us habitually squeeze and compress our throats, which unfortunately affects and impairs our breath, voice, and ability to swallow. The following exercise is designed to improve your ability to control and expand the size of the throat, which results in the release of the deeply held tension within the mouth and around the larynx.

1. Allow yourself to be comfortable . . . either lying down or sitting up with your back, neck, and spine fully supported. Knowing that you will not be interrupted for the next little while, begin by gently closing your eyes.

2. Now begin to bring your attention to your breath—the direct experience of your breath— however it is . . . and however it changes. Allow yourself to softly focus your awareness on to the breath that is arising right now . . . the in-breath and the out-breath . . . the rising and the falling. If you can, try to follow one full cycle of the breath from the beginning of the in-breath and through its entirety to the beginning of the out-breath and through its entirety. Allow yourself the time and the space to be in direct contact with the breath throughout one entire cycle.

3. Now begin to focus attention on the space inside your mouth. Allow yourself to sense or visualize the space that runs down your throat and into your lungs.

4. Begin gently and slowly to squeeze the muscles of your throat and mouth, making them tighter and tighter, creating more and more tension. Notice as the tension expands and spreads into your neck, shoulders, and face.

5. Keeping your lips tightly pursed, begin to reverse the process by gently relaxing all of the muscles in and around your mouth and throat. Expand the space, allowing more and more.

6. Continue to alternately tighten and loosen the muscles, expanding and collapsing the space inside.

7. Now, with the space in your mouth closed, lips tightly pursed and your throat constricted, attempt to vocalize sounds. Begin with your name or "Hello." Pay attention to quality of the sounds that you make. Notice the vibrational difference between your normal speech and this constricted one.

8. Now, once again, rest for a moment, and once again return your attention to the breath that is arising right now . . . the in-breath and the out-breath . . . the rising and the falling. Allow yourself the time and the space to be in direct contact with this one breath throughout its entire cycle.

9. Once again begin to expand your throat and repeat the same sounds or words. Notice the difference in the sound. Notice the difference in your chest, shoulders, and neck, as well as your jaw and face.

10. Continue to alternate between expanding and constricting your throat, while experimenting with different sounds until you've developed not only awareness but conscious control over the habitual pattern of constriction and tension.

Mantra Meditation

WHAT IS A MANTRA?

The word *mantra* itself comes from India and means a "mental device," or a technique to calm and center the mind. Mantras, which are chants or prayers, are believed to have a sacred meaning and power. Although they come in various shapes and sizes, they should be kept relatively short to make repetition as easy as possible. They might be one sentence, a few short sentences, single words, or even single syllables. They can be any word that has meaning for you. For obvious reasons, single-syllable mantras, also known as seed mantras, are the easiest to remember and recite. "Om" and "RAM" are two of the oldest and most widely known of these seed mantras.

The power of mantras is widely recognized in the East and presently, due to the explosion of brain imaging techniques, gaining attention here in the West. Italian researchers discovered that this type of recitation regulated the breath and synchronized the heart rhythms of 23 participants, producing physiological benefits to the heart. The researchers speculated that this happened due to the slowed down breath rate (to the optimal rate of six breaths per minute). Silently repeating a mantra did not produce the same effects as reciting them out loud. It appears that the vocal recitations engage the breath rhythms that, in turn, influence the heart rhythms via the central nervous system. Smoothing and lengthening the breath regulates heart rhythms, oxygenates the blood, and induces a feeling of calmness and well-being.

For this exercise, you will begin by choosing a word or phrase that holds meaning or significance to you. For most people, this is the most difficult part, so to help, here are some examples that others have used. You may use one of these or feel free to choose your own. Whatever works for you.

OM

AUM

RAM

OM MANE PADME HUM

WAHE GURU

KYRIE ELEISON

JESUS

ALLAH HU

Once you've chosen a word or phrase, take a restful, seated pose. With your back straight, and head, neck, and spine aligned, allow your body to relax as completely as possible.

Close your eyes or choose a spot on which to focus your gaze. Take a deep cleansing breath, followed by another deep inhalation. On the exhale, begin to repeat your mantra silently. After three silent recitations, begin to vocalize the mantra.

Repeat it in a gentle, soft, open voice, without any particular emphasis, and in no particular tone. With smooth, relaxed, and even breaths, continue to repeat your mantra.

As you repeat your mantra, bring your attention to the quality of the sound. Listen closely, as if you were listening to it on the radio, giving careful attention to each and every repetition of each and every syllable.

Each time that you notice your attention has wandered, gently and repeatedly bring it back to the sound of the mantra. Again and again, gently bring your attention back to the sound.

Continue for three to five minutes. Notice the change in your body as well as your mind as both become increasingly calm and centered.

KOTO-DAMA: THE SPIRIT OF WORDS FROM DÖ-IN

According to *The Book of Dö-In*, the practice of proper pronunciation of certain sounds are known to alter physiological, emotional, cognitive, and spiritual conditions. The following examples may be used in daily practice to strengthen not only one's physical condition, but mental and spiritual as well. When spoken from a condition of health, each spoken syllable carries its own respective meaning and power. Some sounds are pronounced with an open mouth (*yin* sounds), while others are pronounced with the mouth closed (*yang* sounds). There are many variations in between.

These basic sounds have been pronounced since ancient times in the East:

The vowels in the sounds below are pronounced as follows:									
"A" as in "**Ah**" "E" as in "**They**"			"U" as in "**True**" "O" as in "**Rose**"			"I" as in "**Machine**"			
A	KA	SA	TA	NA	HA	MA	YA	RA	WA
I	KI	SHI	CHI	NI	HI	MI	I	RI	I
U	KU	SU	TSU	NU	FU	MU	YU	RU	U
E	KE	SE	TE	NE	HE	ME	E	RE	E
O	KO	SO	TO	NO	HO	MO	YO	RO	O

These 50 sounds vibrate certain parts of the body (e.g., "I" activates the stomach and middle region of the body; "O" the kidneys and the back side of the middle region; "HA" more for the lungs and respiratory function). Some examples frequently used in Dö-In exercises are:

- The prolonged sound of "SU." This sound is for harmony between ourselves and all others. In our breathing, we sound "SU" in exhaling, with or without actually uttering the sound. Breathing is the medium harmonizing ourselves with our surroundings.

- The prolonged sound of "A-U-M." The sound "A," which is pronounced with the mouth open, represents the infinite universe, and physically it vibrates the lower part of our body. The sound "U" represents harmony, as we saw in the case of the sound "SU," and it physically vibrates the upper region of the body and the lower region of the head. The sound "M," which is pronounced with the mouth closed, represents the infinitesimal world and physically vibrates the most compacted area of the brain. Therefore, if we pronounce "A-U-M," it is the expression of the whole universe and vibrates our body and spiritual channel from the lowest part to the highest part, resulting in the active charge of vibrations and electromagnetic currents in our physical, mental, and spiritual functions.

- A series of sounds: "NAM-MYO-HO-REN-GE-KYO." This series of sounds has been used in one of the Buddhist sects as a chant and prayer. The meaning of this chant is: *"Infinite Miraculous Law of the Lotus Flower Sutra,"* or *"The Miraculous Order of the Infinite Universe,"* the teaching of which has been considered as the ultimate essential teaching of Buddhism.

Kirtan Kriya

Kirtan Kriya is a meditation somatic and chant exercise originating from Kundalini yoga.

At the Amen Clinics*, they performed a single-photon emission computed tomography (SPECT) study on people using this particular of type of meditation. They scanned 11 people on one day when they didn't meditate and then the next day during a meditation session. The brain imaging scans taken after the meditation showed a significant increase in activity in the prefrontal cortex, the area of the brain associated with executive function, fear inhibition, attention span, and thoughtfulness, as well as increased activity in the right temporal lobe, the area of the brain associated with spirituality.

INSTRUCTIONS:

Take a restful, seated pose on the floor or in a chair. With your back straight and head, neck, and spine aligned, allow your body to relax as completely as possible. Close your eyes or choose a spot on which to focus your gaze. Rest your hands on your knees with palms up. Take a deep cleansing breath, followed by another deep inhalation. With your hands in the following mudras, chant the syllables *Sah, Tah, Nah, Mah.* Lengthen the ending of each sound as you repeat: Sah . . . Tah . . . Nah . . . Mah.

1. Touch your index finger tip to the tip of your thumb as you chant:
   Saaaaaaaahh.

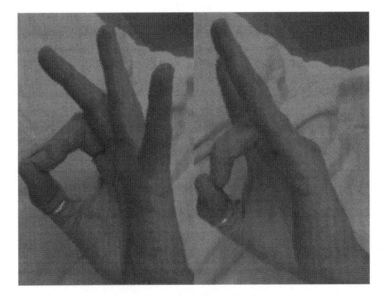

2. Touch your middle finger tip to the tip of your thumb as you chant:
   Taaaaaaaahh.

---

*Amen Clinics, Inc., specializes in brain health and innovative diagnosis and treatment for a wide variety of neuropsychiatric, behavioral, and learning problems among children, teenagers, and adults. Established in 1989 by Dr. Daniel Amen, the center has a national reputation for utilizing brain SPECT imaging for a wide variety of neuropsychiatric problems, including ADD, anxiety, depression, autism, and memory problems.

3. Touch your ring finger tip to the tip of your thumb as you chant:
Naaaaaaaahh.

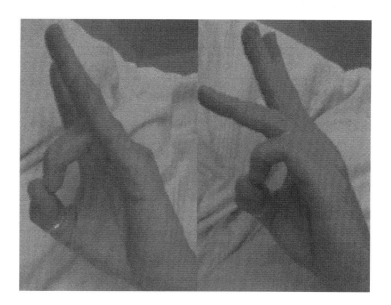

4. Touch your pinky tip to the tip of your thumb as you chant:
Maaaaaaaahh.

Do the finger movements shown in the preceding steps as you chant in the following sequence:

- Chant out loud for 2 minutes.
- Chant in a whisper for 2 minutes.
- Chant in silence for 4 minutes.
- Chant in a whisper for 2 minutes.
- Chant out loud for 2 minutes.

Shoulder Gripping Chant

This intervention is multifaceted in its effects. By extending and lengthening the neck muscles, it relieves muscular tension. By physically vibrating the upper region of the body and the lower region of the head, it is said to create harmony. By reeducating the proprioception of the neck and shoulder muscles, it improves auditory skills. The net effect is an overall improvement in attention, focus, and memory.

INSTRUCTIONS:

1. In a comfortable seated position, begin by inhaling, as you bring your shoulders up and back.

2. On the exhale, relax your shoulders while keeping the spine elongated.

3. Using your left hand, grasp and hold the top of the right shoulder. Begin to exert a firm pressure on the muscle groups in and around the area.

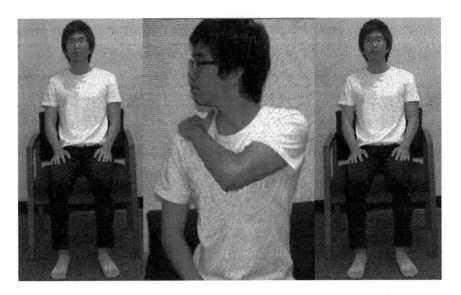

4. While gripping the muscles, slowly and gently rotate your head as far to the right as it will comfortably go (i.e., without excessively straining).

5. With your head turned and your eyes gazing over your right shoulder, inhale gently and fully, allowing your chest to open and your spine to continue to lengthen.

6. With your lips puckered and slightly opened, exhale while chanting the sound "U" as in "True." At the end of the exhalation, once again inhale deeply and again exhale while chanting the sound "U" as in "True."

7. Return your head to center position and relax your arms.

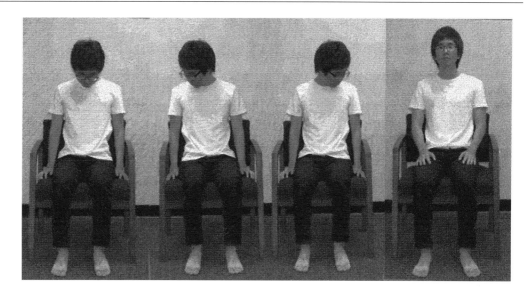

8. Breathing normally, drop your head toward your chest, tuck your chin and relax your shoulders, and remain here for one or two breaths.

9. Continue breathing normally as you turn your head to the right, then the left.

10. Return your head to center position.

11. Begin again by inhaling, as you bring your shoulders up and back.

12. On the exhale, relax your shoulders while keeping the spine elongated.

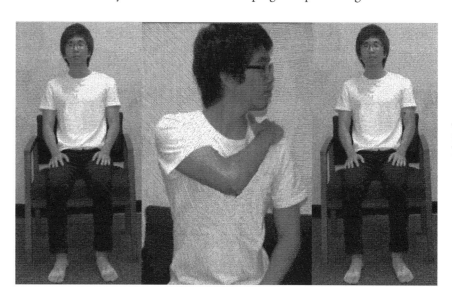

13. Using your right hand, grasp and hold the top of the left shoulder. Begin to exert a firm pressure on the muscle group in and around the area.

14. While gripping the muscles, slowly and gently rotate your head as far to the left as it will comfortably go (i.e., without excessively straining).

15. With your head turned and your eyes gazing over your left shoulder, inhale gently and fully, allowing your chest to open and your spine to continue to lengthen. With your lips puckered and slightly opened, exhale while chanting the sound "U" as in "True." At the end of the exhalation, once again inhale deeply and again exhale while chanting the sound "U" as in "True."

16. Return your head to center position and relax your arms.

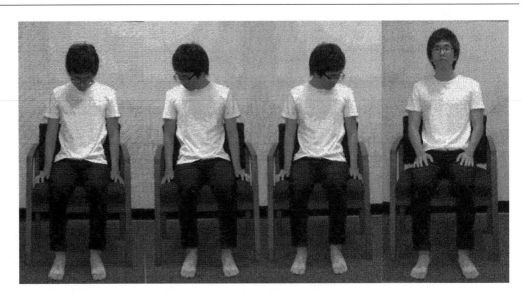

17. Breathing normally once again, drop your head toward your chest, tuck your chin and relax your shoulders, and remain here for one or two breaths.

18. Return your head to center position.

Discerning Intention

in·ten·tion (*noun*)

1. An act or instance of determining mentally upon some action or result.
2. Purpose or attitude toward the effect of one's actions or conduct.

Intention is the force directing an *act of will*. One must be aware of his/her own genuine intentions in order to take responsibility for the consequences of his/her actions.

IMAGERY EXERCISE

The following is a simple but effective technique for contemplating and discerning one's genuine intention. It has three parts: a guided imagery script, a follow-up worksheet, and an embodied commitment.

INSTRUCTIONS:

1. Read the following imagery script.

   Allow yourself to be comfortable . . . either lying down or sitting up with your back, neck, and spine fully supported. Knowing that you will not be interrupted for the next little while, begin by gently closing your eyes. . . . Now begin to bring your attention to your breath—the direct experience of your breath—however it is . . . and however it changes. Allow yourself to softly focus your awareness on the breath that is arising right now . . . the in-breath and the out-breath . . . the rising and the falling. If you can, try to follow one full cycle of the breath from the beginning of the in-breath and through its entirety to the beginning of the out-breath and through its entirety. Allow yourself the time and the space to be in direct contact with the breath throughout one entire cycle.

   As you continue to pay attention to the breath, you may notice that many, many distractions arise. Just allow yourself to notice those distractions and any bodily sensations or any thoughts that may arise. If possible allow yourself to become aware of the separateness of these bodily sensations—notice how these sensations are separate, distinct from thoughts, ideas, and words.

   Now, if you will, bring yourself psychologically to the end of your life, not in a frightening or threatening way, but in a contemplative way, as if you are considering the message or moral at the end of your story. Begin to examine your values and your successes. Now, if you will, with great compassion understanding, and forgiveness, begin to consider how you might have done a better job of living out your personal values. Perhaps you might have done better for yourself and for others. Use this gentle consideration from that future place to uncover what this *future you* might say to the *present you*: What brings meaning to your life? What is your true purpose? How could you better fulfill that purpose?

   After time for contemplation, return to this room. Gently open your eyes. Take a few conscious, cleansing breaths.

2. Summon as much compassion for yourself as possible, and continue on to the worksheet.

    Now, using a mirror or talking with a friend, explain what you have written on the worksheet and what it means to you. Whether using a friend or a mirror, no response is needed, Just listen.

3. Finally, come to a standing position, come into fully embodied awareness. Once established in this empowered stance, bring to mind one of your intentions, perhaps the one that is easiest to realize.

    Now, bring to mind the opposite side of this intention (i.e., what might stand in the way).

    Carefully consider this obstacle, then bring to mind the decision to act despite the presence of an obstacle.

    Becoming fully cognizant of your strengths, consider how much it would benefit you and others if your intention were realized.

    Now, becoming fully and entirely aware of the other side, try to completely understand its opposite position and how you can appease its needs reasonably without renouncing your intention.

    Finally, allow yourself to open to the universe. Consider the consequences of your intention and appraise whether it would truly increase the good of all. Fully examine your intentionality. When you are sure that your intentions are sound, make the decision on what first step you will take.

WORKSHEET: LIFE'S PURPOSE/CORE VALUES

My life's purpose is:

_____

_____

_____

_____

_____

My personal guidelines for living well in the world are:

_____

_____

_____

_____

_____

Core values that reflect this purpose are (e.g., if your life's purpose is to advocate for the less fortunate, you might write "compassion," "courage," "generosity," etc.):

_____

_____

_____

_____

_____

One instance in which my core values(s) made a difference in my life was:

_____

_____

_____

_____

_____

Using your core values as intentions, list the concrete actions and necessary behaviors to realize these intentions (e.g., if your life's purpose is to advocate for the less fortunate the necessary behaviors might be working with a charitable organization, donating time and money, etc.).

The concrete actions to accomplish these intentions are:

_____

_____

_____

_____

_____

An Action Plan: "Willingness"

My (specific) goal is to:

_____

_____

_____

_____

_____

The values underlying my goal are:

_____

_____

_____

_____

_____

The (specific) actions I will take to achieve that goal are:

1. _____

2. _____

3. _____

4. _____

In pursuit of my goal, I am willing to open up to and make space for all of these memories, thoughts, feelings, bodily sensations, longings . . .

Memories:

_____

_____

Thoughts:

_____

_____

_____

Feelings:

_____

_____

Sensations:

_____

_____

Longings, needs, and urges:

_____

_____

It might be useful to remind myself that:

_____

_____

If necessary, I can break this goal down into more manageable steps, such as:

1. _____

2. _____

3. _____

The smallest, easiest step I can begin with is:

_____

_____

I will begin on _____/_____/_____ @ _____:_____ (I will take the first step.)

WORKSHEET: IMPORTANT QUESTIONS

A Writing Exercise

WHO I AM

Today I am . . .

_____

_____

_____

_____

Yesterday I was . . .

_____

_____

_____

_____

In the past I have been . . .

_____

_____

_____

_____

I am becoming . . .

_____

_____

_____

_____

I define my identity as . . .

_____

_____

_____

_____

I am known by all of these names . . .

_____

_____

_____

_____

The parts of myself that I reveal to others are . . .

_____

_____

_____

_____

The parts of myself that I conceal are . . .

_____

_____

_____

_____

I have worn masks and played many roles. The ones that I have worn and since discarded are . . .

_____

_____

_____

_____

I would define my authentic self as . . .

_____

_____

_____

_____

I share my true self with . . .

_____

_____

_____

_____

WHY I'M HERE

My purpose for being in this place right now is . . .

_____

_____

_____

_____

I have to learn . . .

_____

_____

_____

_____

I have to teach . . .

_____

_____

_____

_____

The following experiences in my recent past have prepared me to be here . . .

_____

_____

_____

_____

This is how I got here . . .

_____

_____

_____

_____

Do I want to stay here?

_____

_____

_____

_____

Where do I want to go next?

_____

_____

_____

_____

What does this present moment offer me?

_____

_____

_____

_____

What do I bring to the present moment?

_____

_____

_____

_____

WHAT I WANT

For myself, I want . . .

_____

_____

_____

_____

For others, I want . . .

_____

_____

_____

_____

_____

This is what I want to do . . .

_____

_____

_____

_____

_____

I want to be . . .

_____

_____

_____

_____

I want to have . . .

_____

_____

_____

_____

The most important thing for me to do is . . .

_____

_____

_____

_____

In order to do this, I need to have . . .

_____

_____

_____

_____

In order to do this, I need to know . . .

_____

_____

_____

_____

In order to do this, I need to do . . .

_____

_____

_____

_____

Do I have what I want?

_____

_____

_____

_____

Do I want what I have?

_____

_____

_____

WORKSHEET: THINGS YOU MIGHT NOT KNOW ABOUT ME

Couples

Both people should answer the following questions. The information is then shared and processed, usually within a couple's session.

1. What do I need to do or be in order not to engrave "*if only . . .*" on my gravestone?

   _____

   _____

   _____

   _____

2. If I could change only one thing in my life, what would that be and why?

   _____

   _____

   _____

   _____

3. In what settings am I the happiest/eager/most comfortable?

   _____

   _____

   _____

   _____

4. In what settings am I the saddest/unsure/afraid?

   _____

   _____

   _____

   _____

5. In a typical day, what do I find myself thinking about the most?

_____

_____

_____

_____

_____

6. What do I feel is my greatest accomplishment to date? Was it done alone, or were others involved?

_____

_____

_____

_____

7. Presently, what major regret do I have in my life? If it is reparable, what would be required to repair it?

_____

_____

_____

_____

8. What other things do I want to change now, and why?

_____

_____

_____

_____

9. Who was my best friend in grade school, in high school, in college, and why?

_____

_____

_____

_____

10. Of all the people I have ever known, read about, or dreamed of, who is the worst, and why?

_____

_____

_____

_____

11. Of all the people I have ever known, read about, or dreamed of, who is most heroic, and why?

_____

_____

_____

_____

Full Awareness

Zen-based meditation is focused on bringing awareness of the sensations, thoughts, actions, and emotions, without getting involved or analyzing them. In other words, you stand witness to the things that happen in and around you (in the service of developing an observing self).

Here is a story that illustrates the essence of Zen meditation:

After ten years of apprenticeship, Tenno achieved the rank of Zen teacher. One rainy day, he went to visit the famous master Nan-in. When he walked in, the master greeted him with a question, "Did you leave your wooden clogs and umbrella on the porch?"

"Yes," Tenno replied.

"Tell me," the master continued, "did you place your umbrella to the left of your shoes, or to the right?"

Tenno did not know the answer and realized that he had not yet attained full awareness. So he became Nan-in's apprentice and studied under him for ten more years. (Suler, 2012)

Awareness is also one of the pillars of Gestalt therapy.

In *The Gestalt Therapy Book*, Joel Latner writes:

> The kingpin of the Gestalt methodology is awareness. The task of therapy is to examine the structure of our experience, finding out what it is we experience, and how we do it. In contrast to approaches that are concerned with understanding why we behave as we do, Gestalt therapy is interested in finding out what we do, and how we do it. Introspection and an historical curiosity are replaced by an experiential examination of the structure and function of behavior. "To dissolve a neurotic system, one needs awareness of the symptom, not explanations; just as to dissolve a piece of sugar one needs water, not philosophy."

> The purpose of these techniques is to bring our present existence to our awareness. By paying attention to ourself, we come to know that our actual experience is. This is a reversal of impaired functioning. In the latter, we are intent on avoiding aspects of our existence. In therapy, attending to our experience instead, we confront our life instead of avoiding it. In therapy, we encourage our health by being healthy. We move toward the goal of living in the present by living in the present and examining it, by being aware of ourself, our awareness, our situation, our existence.

> To focus on awareness means, again, that the here-and-now, our existence, and our experience are central. In Gestalt therapy we are not historians or symbolists. We are existentialists, phenomenologists, working in the present moment. ...

> What is available in the present to the therapy is what we can be in touch with: our movements, gestures, speech, feelings, posture, our expressions, our interactions with

reality. Working in the present, we deal with what is in front of us, the surface of behavior. This is one of the major characteristics of the Gestalt methodology, that it is oriented to the surface of behavior. It deals not with the deepest recesses of the unconscious but the obviousness of present functioning. "Obvious," from the Latin, and "problem," from the Greek, have the same root meaning: in the way. ***What is in your way is what is in front of you*** (pp. 109–111).

The next series of exercises borrow from both the Zen tradition and Gestalt therapy principles.

Roots Meditation

GROUNDING EXERCISE

The following exercise is adapted from Reginald Ray's conception of "Earth Breathing."

INSTRUCTIONS:

Recite imagery script:

Lie on your back in a comfortable position, with your back, neck, and spine fully supported. Knowing that you will not be interrupted for next little while, begin by gently closing your eyes.

Now begin to bring your attention to your breath—the direct experience of your breath— however it is . . . and however it changes. Allow yourself to softly focus your awareness on to the breath that is arising right now . . . the in-breath and the out-breath . . . the rising and the falling. If you can, try to follow one full cycle of the breath from the beginning of the in-breath and through its entirety to the beginning of the out-breath and through its entirety. Allow yourself the time and the space to be in direct contact with the breath throughout one entire cycle.

Now, if you will, just allow your awareness to drop down into the Earth. Feel your consciousness sinking into the ground beneath you.

At first, drop down just about a foot or two. Begin to imagine that you have roots that go down into the ground. Feel these roots connecting you to the earth.

Next, allow your consciousness to drop down a bit more, perhaps 8 to 10 feet down into the Earth. Becoming aware of your roots extending further into the ground, feel the strength, solidity, and warmth of the Earth.

- 100 feet. Keep dropping further into the earth: 300, 400, etc.
- 1,000 feet. Keep dropping down into the earth: 2,000, 3,000, 4,000, etc.

Now, allow your consciousness to drop down a mile into the Earth. Let go of any resistances, and once again open your awareness to this depth.

With each breath, allow your consciousness to drop down another 10 miles into the Earth, until you reach 100 miles. Feel yourself well down into the earth now.

Now, in awareness, continue to simply drop, deeper and deeper. If you should run into any barriers or resistance, just allow yourself to move through or around it—dropping deeper and deeper toward the Earth's center.

Even though the physical Earth has a limited depth, the depth of this experiential Earth is infinite. Allow yourself to continue to drop, or be pulled toward, the infinite depth of the Earth. Imagine this infinite depth as the source or origin of all things. This source is your true home.

Keep dropping, or allow yourself to be pulled downward by your desire and longing for your true home, the source of being. Keep opening, letting go of any resistance, Keep descending.

Bring your attention to your body. Notice its contact with the infinite depth of the Earth. Your body is getting extremely relaxed down here.

Rest here at the point of infinity beneath you. Here, you can let go of all concepts, all thoughts, and all ideas. Just be. With the infinity beneath you, let go of any effort. This is the point of total relaxation. Notice your experience here—unbounded and completely open . . . no barriers, restrictions, or boundaries.

Remain here as long as you like.

According to Salzberg (2010):

> "The four steps in dealing with an emotion mindfully—recognition, acceptance, investigation, and nonidentification (some teachers of mediation like to use the acronym RAIN)—can also be applied to thoughts. We tend to identify with our thoughts in a way we don't identify with our bodies. When we're feeling blue and thinking lots of sorrowful thoughts, we say to ourselves, I am a sad person. But if we bang our funny bone, we don't usually say to ourselves I am a sore elbow. Most of the times, we think we are our thoughts. We forget, or have never noticed, that there's an aspect of our mind that's watching these thoughts arise and pass away. The point of mindfulness is to get in touch with that witnessing capacity. Sometimes I ask students to imagine each thought as a visitor knocking at the door of their house. The thoughts don't live there; you can greet them, acknowledge them, and watch them go.
>
> Mindfulness practice isn't meant to eliminate thinking but rather to help us know what we're thinking when we're thinking it, just as we want to know what we're feeling when we're feeling it.
>
> Mindfulness allows us to watch our thoughts, see how one thought leads to the next, decide if we're heading down an unhealthy path, and, if so, let go and change directions. It allows us to see that who we are is much more than a fearful or envious or angry thought. We can rest in the awareness of the thought, in the compassion we extend to ourselves if the thought makes us uncomfortable, and in the balance and good sense we summon as we decide whether and how to act on the thought." (pps 110-111)

Mindfulness need not be a formal meditation. In fact, cultivating mindfulness is something that can—and probably should—be practiced throughout the activities of daily living. This practice is simple, but simple does not mean easy!

A SIMPLE PRACTICE (GROUP OR INDIVIDUAL)

INSTRUCTIONS:

1. Begin with a conscious intention to set aside five minutes several times each day for a week or two to check in with yourself. Initially you will probably need a reminder, so perhaps for the first week or two you might choose specific times for the exercise.

2. During these five-minute intervals, you will be doing an inquiry. Ask yourself, "What is going on right now?" In your answer, include any awarenesses that are present; include

thoughts, sensations, movements, feelings, and the surroundings. If and when self-judgments arise, notice them, but quickly let them go as you return to the inquiry into your immediate embodied experience.

For example: "I am standing in line. My left foot is resting on top of my right foot. My left forearm is itchy. My head feels heavy. My breath is uneven and shallow. My thoughts are scattered. I must be doing this wrong because I'm uncomfortable. I notice that this is a judgment. Again, I'm noticing that I feel warm. The lights seem very bright. Now, my breath has gotten a little bit deeper. . . ."

As this form of inquiry becomes easier, increase the number of times that you check in. Eventually, this type of inquiry no longer feels disruptive or effortful.

Walking Meditation

GROUP

This exercise is exactly as labeled: *a mindful walk.*

INSTRUCTIONS:

- Begin to walk slowly and deliberately. Bring a soft focus to your breath—however it is . . . and however it changes. The breath becomes the anchor . . . the point of return. With your focus on the breath that is arising right now, begin to allow your mind to become aware of the sights, sounds, or physical sensations that arise.
- Focus your awareness for a moment on that sight, sound, or sensation, and then return your awareness to your breath.
- As distractions (thoughts, memories, plans, etc.) arise (and they will), simply notice them and then allow each to dissolve. . . . Now, very gently, refocus your awareness on your breath.
- After a few minutes, stop walking.
- Find a place to sit down and write about this experience.
- The facilitator should instruct participants to break up into small groups. Present each group with the following questions:
  - What thoughts, memories, or associations came up during the walk?
  - Was there a persistent theme?
  - Describe the sensory experience during the walk:
    - What did you see during the walk?
    - What sounds did you notice during the walk?
    - What smells did you notice?
    - What physical sensations did you notice (e.g., breeze or wind, the texture of the ground, temperature of anything (s)he touched, and the various tactile and kinesthetic sensations associated with walking)? What internal feelings came up during the walk? What was your "felt sense" of the experience? What did you notice about the rest of the group during the walk (e.g., who was positioned where, who led, who followed, did subgroups develop, or were people on their own, etc.)?

After the small group discussion, ask participants to become aware of their own particular type of sensory experience. For example, was it more visual? Auditory? Kinesthetic and/or tactile sensations? Additionally, ask questions regarding the degree to which each was attuned to his/her own internal world of thoughts, feelings, and memories.

Ask to what degree each was attuned to the social aspect.

Mindfulness Eating Exercise

GROUP OR INDIVIDUAL (*USING A GRAPE, RAISIN OR HERSHEY KISS*)

(Adapted from Kabat-Zinn and McWatters, *Full Catastrophe Living*, 2009.)

Throughout the entirety of this observational exercise, remain vigilantly aware of your own bodily sensations, thoughts, memories, and associations that come to mind. Notice when your awareness fluctuates, drifts away, or is interrupted (e.g., when your thoughts take you into the future, such as making plans or judgments like "this is silly!").

INSTRUCTIONS:

Have participants select a grape, raisin, or Hershey Kiss from a plate. Once each participant has chosen his/her food item, the facilitator will read the following (or some version of it):

"So, being from another planet and all, you have obviously never seen anything like this before, but you are satisfied that it is, in fact, food. Because you are observing it for the first time, you will want to study it carefully. Pick it up, feel its weight and temperature. Begin to inspect its exterior, taking notice of its shape, color, texture, and anything else interesting about it. . . . Now, bring the item closer to your nose and begin to smell it. Try to fully comprehend the smell of this item. And while keeping its smell in the forefront of your awareness, check in with your body, noticing any reactions you may be having to the smell. . . . Now, bring your awareness to your dominant hand. Using the dominant hand, bring the item to your mouth. Place it in your mouth, but do not chew or swallow it yet. First, become aware of its textures . . . and flavor or flavors. Explore the sensations of holding this item in your mouth . . . on your tongue. . . . As slowly as possible, begin to experience its taste as you bite into it and begin to chew. Be fully aware of the sounds and the movements of your mouth as you chew. . . . And when you are ready, swallow. And as you do, continue to sense its taste as it goes down your throat … noticing any tastes that continue to linger … and any sensations that you experience. Continue to observe your experience.

When everyone has finished, the facilitator should present these questions for processing the experience:

- How was that experience for you?
- Was anything surprising about it?
- How did it differ from the way you typically eat?
- Is there some way for you to bring this quality of "awarenessing" into your life?

In her work, *Gestalt Therapy Theory: An Overview*, Maria Kirchner (2000) defines Gestalt therapy and theory as follows:

Gestalt therapy is a well-developed and well-grounded theory with a myriad of tenets, principles, concepts, and methods. . . . Gestalt Therapy is a sound science and a powerful means for facilitating and nurturing the full functioning of the human person with the potential of bringing about human healing, growth, and wholeness. In Perls, Hefferline, and Goodman's (1951/1994) terms, the "Gestalt outlook is the original, undistorted, natural approach to life, to man's [and woman's] thinking, acting, feeling" (p. xxiv). Therefore, the criteria of therapeutic progress are measured against "the patient's own awareness of heightened vitality and more effective functioning" (p. 15). At the end of therapy the client is not necessarily "cured" but able to access tools and equipment to deal with any kind of problems he/she will have to encounter.

BASIC PRINCIPLES OF GESTALT THERAPY THEORY

Gestalt therapy theory holds a nonmaterialistic and antireductionist position that disavows dualistic and linear thinking. Like all psychotherapies, Gestalt therapy is an approach to human change. Change, however, is not directly aimed at but viewed as an inescapable product of contact and awareness, considered together with their interruptions and/or various degrees of absence.

Contact

The essence of human life is contact, a meeting with various kinds of others. Every organism is capable of effective and fulfilling contact with others in their environment and pursues ways of having contact with others so that the organism can survive and grow to maturity. All contact is creative and dynamic and, as such, each experience unfolds as a creative adjustment of the organism in the environment (Perls, Hefferline, and & Goodman, 1951/1994). Contact is the forming of a figure of interest against a ground within the context of the organism-environment field. (see figure,/ground formation and destruction). It is also defined as "the awareness of, and the behavior toward, the assimilable; and the rejection of the unassimilable novelty" (Perls et al., 1951/1994, p. 230). To have the opportunity for functional and existential contacts in the field, as well as the strength to repudiate and/or sustain unhealthy contacts, is the quintessence of growth and change.

Processes of Contact

There are three major ways of conceptualizing the process of contacting, which is in general a sequence of grounds and figures. The four stages of contact were originally described by Perls, Hefferline, and Goodman, (1951), as fore-contact, contacting, final-contact, and post-contact.

Interruptions of Contact

Since Because every contact takes place at the contact boundary, where the organism and the environment meet, every interruption or distortion of contact was/is also called a contact boundary disturbance (Perls et al.), or an interruption of self-regulation (Polster and Polsters). There are four major interruptions of contact, which all result in loss of ego-functions: confluence, introjection, projection, and retroflection. In addition, there are the concepts of egotism (Perls et al., 1951/1994), deflection (Polster& and Polster, 1973), and proflection (Crocker, 1981) are involved. Every interruption reflects the client's organization of his/her experience. Therefore, it is paramount to work towards change in the ground that supports the experience.

- *Confluence*: the condition of no-contact. Instead of an "'I'" and a "'You,'" there is a "'we'" or a vague, unclear experience of him/herself.

- *Introjection*: the individual experiences something as him/herself when in fact it belongs to the environment (false identification).

- *Projection*: the individual experiences something in the environment when in fact it belongs to him/her (false alienation).

- *Retroflection*: the individual holds back a response intended for the environment and substitutes it with a response for him/herself.

Confluence, introjection, projection, and retroflection are often in the service of health and are only detrimental to healthy functioning without awareness (Kirchner, 2000).

"Gestalt Therapy Theory: An Overview." Maria Kirchner in *Gestalt!* 2000, Vol. 3(4): *http://www.g-gej.org/4-3/theoryoverview.html* (with permission)

According to Latner (1973), "In Gestalt Therapy, behavior is characterized. Patterns are underlined. To the extent that they are regular and repeated, the therapist points out the repetition" (p. 138).

In contrast to psychoanalysis's process of "uncovering," Gestalt therapy prefers a more process-oriented, phenomenological approach. Polster and Polster (1973) point out, "We just prefer to follow the freshly unfolding process itself rather than to view the process as uncovering something previously obscured. We would rather bake a pie than look for one" (p. 122). They also posit: "The seven basic contact functions are: talking, moving, seeing, hearing, touching, tasting, and smelling. . . . In focusing on these functions, the Gestalt therapist seeks to improve such qualities as clarity, timing, directness, and flexibility (p. 122).

These seven functions, or contact gates, provide clinicians a cornerstone for organizing the work, so even if the clinician loses the narrative or theme of the work, (s)he can easily fall back on practical questions regarding these basic functions.

The worksheet that follows was adapted from a list developed by Delisle, which is found in *Critical Collaboration: Adlerian Therapy and Gestalt Therapy* (Savard, 2011) and is based on the contact functions described earlier. Its purpose is to provide clinicians with a subjective assessment of clients' contact functions, which may prove helpful during initial (and subsequent) assessments.

ASSESSMENT OF CONTACT FUNCTIONS

VOICE/SPEECH CONTACT FUNCTION

1. How would I describe this person's voice?

   _____

   _____

   _____

   _____

2. What do I feel in response to this voice?

   _____

   _____

   _____

   _____

3. What emotions do I imagine this voice best expresses?

   _____

   _____

   _____

   _____

4. How does this person use his/her voice?

   _____

   _____

   _____

   _____

TOUCH/MOVEMENT CONTACT FUNCTION

1. What do I imagine I would feel if this person touched me?

   _____

   _____

   _____

2. What do I imagine each of us would feel if we were to touch?

_____

_____

_____

_____

3. Would I like to touch him/her?

_____

_____

_____

4. How does this person use his/her body in relation to space?

_____

_____

_____

_____

5. Are his/her movements fluid, controlled, or rigid?

_____

_____

_____

_____

6. How does this person use the furniture (floor, pillows, etc.) in terms of support?

_____

_____

_____

_____

7. How does the person move?

_____

_____

_____

LOOKING/SEEING CONTACT FUNCTION

1. When does the client look at me?

_____

_____

_____

2. When does the client look away from me?

_____

_____

_____

3. How do I feel about the way in which the client looks at me?

_____

_____

_____

4. How would I describe this person's eyes and the way in which they look?

_____

_____

_____

5. What emotions do I feel that these eyes would most easily express?

_____

_____

_____

_____

6. What are my visceral reactions to being looked at by this client?

_____

_____

_____

_____

LISTENING/HEARING CONTACT FUNCTION

1. Does this person appear to hear me with ease, or does (s)he seem to struggle to hear me?

_____

_____

_____

2. Does this person hear what I am actually saying, or does (s)he hear something else?

_____

_____

_____

3. Do I feel that I am easily heard and understood by this person?

_____

_____

_____

_____

APPEARANCE

1. How would I describe this client's features?

_____

_____

_____

2. Which features stand out for me (e.g., stiff upper body, tight or locked jaw, jittery legs, ever-moving hands, frozen expression, etc.)?

_____

_____

_____

_____

3. How would I describe the client's manner of dressing?

_____

_____

_____

_____

4. What is my impression of his/her overall level of self-care?

_____

_____

_____

_____

Developing Presence Exercise

GROUP OR COUPLES

(Adapted from Claudio Naranjo, *Gestalt Therapy: The Attitude & Practice of Atheoretical Experientialism*, 1993.) For further information regarding Dr. Naranjo's work, please visit: www.naranjoinstitute.org.uk

INSTRUCTIONS:

PART ONE: *I-NESS*

Begin in pairs with participants sitting face to face with one another. Instruct each dyad to begin by closing their eyes and bringing attention to their bodies—bodily sensations, postures, and facial expressions. Invite each to adjust his/her posture or attitude in any way that they like.

Instruct them as follows: "In this moment, be as you are; be as you like; be as you want to be . . . in this moment . . . in this moment."

After a short while, instruct each to remain in body and thought as is, but to gently open his/her eyes, begin to bring relaxation to his/her eyes.

Say: "Now, begin to relax your body, allowing yourself to remain at ease. Without trying to do anything or make anything special happen, allow your mind to grow quiet as you bring your full attention to the "felt sense" of existing . . . feeling and sensing these words 'I am here.'"

"After a short while, of sensing 'I am here,' bring your attention back to the breath while gently shifting your attention from 'I' to 'here' and mentally repeat 'I—am—here' in synchrony with in-breath, pause, and out-breath."

Continue with as much continuity of attention as possible.

PART TWO: *YOU-NESS*

While still in pairs, continue to have participants sitting face to face with one another.

Each dyad should begin the second part of this exercise by closing their eyes and once again bringing attention to their bodies—sensations, postures, and facial expressions. Invite each to adjust his/her posture or attitude in any way that they like.

Continue: "While you sit, physically relaxed and centered—engaging in neither verbal nor nonverbal dialogue—forget yourself as much as possible while you focus on the sense that the person in front of you truly exists. This is a person and not a thing, a conscious being seeing you."

PART THREE: *I/YOU*

While still in pairs, continue with participants sitting face to face with one another.

Each dyad should begin the third and final part of this exercise by closing their eyes, once again bringing attention to their bodies—sensations, postures, and facial expressions. Instruct the dyad to continue to sustain mental silence with open eyes and with the support of physical relaxation, concentration on both "I" and "you," while at the same time evoking a sense of infinity around them. Have each attempt to intensify both the sense of presence of *Self* and *Other* and a sense of cosmic depth. Invite them to allow the sense of the infinite to support their relaxation and dissolve the mind. You may wish to invoke the thought: *I—You—Infinity.*

Exploring Dreams

A GESTALT APPROACH

Fritz Perls described dreams as 'the royal road to integration' (1970). He viewed them as essentially projections in that everything contained in the dream was but a representation of some facet of the dreamer. Consequently, his style of working with dreams followed the methodology of working with projection. This method involves the client talking in the first person from different aspects of the dream, possibly dialoguing with other aspects of the dream.

The common ground for whatever way we work with a dream is that it is viewed as an integration of distinct parts of the self. The starting point for working with a dream is usually to increase the immediacy of sharing the dream by inviting the client to speak as if (s)he is presently in the dream presently (i.e., *first person* using *here-and-now* language, rather than reporting, for example, "I remember there were some police officers in a crazy blue building . . ."). State in the *first person*, and as if it were happening *now*, "I'm in this crazy blue building, there are police officers to my left and now there are some in front of me, coming toward me. . . ."

Encourage the client to stay with the process of the dream and the telling of the dream rather than the content. Remind the client to notice bodily sensations when relating the dream.

EXPLORATION QUESTIONS

- Where would you like to begin?
- What was the immediate feeling when you awoke?
- What is the mood of the dream?
- What reaction(s) did and does it evoke?
- What was your sense of the dream or the dream's meaning?

After the client relates his/her first person's account of the dream, have the client choose an important character in the dream, and then, using here-and-now language, relate the dream from his/her perspective.

- Repeat for any important characters.
- Although there may be resistance to this one, invite the client to choose an inanimate object in the dream and relate the dream from its perspective.
- After the dream has been told from different perspectives, process any of the client's insights with regards to both the dream and relating of the dream.

Further options for exploration include:

- Reenacting the dream in a group psychodrama (see page 137).
- Like all unfinished business, unfinished dreams may be continued in therapy beyond the point of "and then I woke up." The client might be invited to continue in the first person.
- The dream might be expressed through body movement or taking up different postures.

JUNG'S SHADOW SELF

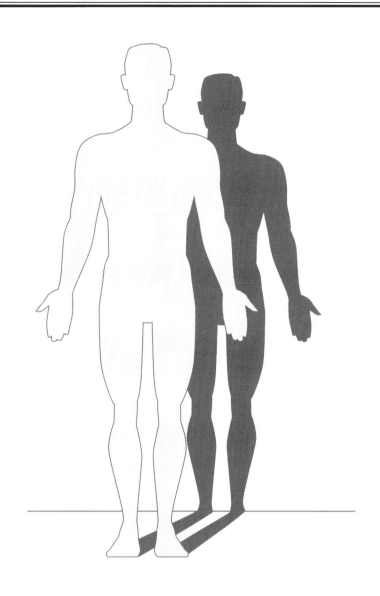

The Shadow Self

The shadow represents traits deep within oneself. Although generally hidden, the shadow self is extremely important to know—and to know deeply. When asked by a reader of his website about "healing the shadow," Deepak Chopra responded:

> We are all aware of having dark impulses, which include hatred, fear, and aggression. These impulses arise from the unconscious, and our normal response is to keep them there. We push the dark side out of sight, yet it doesn't go away. It seeks expression, as all energies will. Healing isn't possible when dark energies are kept bottled inside."

> (http://www.sharecare.com/question/healing-shadow-self)

Carl Jung identified key figures that the archetypes can take. The three of importance here are the Persona, the Shadow, and the Self. As Jung posits:

> Good does not become better by being exaggerated, but worse, and a small evil becomes a big one through being disregarded and repressed. The Shadow is very much a part of human nature, and it is only at night that no Shadows exist. . . . The Shadow is a moral problem that challenges the whole ego-personality, for no one can become conscious of the Shadow without considerable moral effort. To become conscious of it involves recognizing the dark aspects of the personality as present and real. This act is the essential condition for any kind of self-knowledge. (1945, p. 14)

Jung continues:

> A man who is unconscious of himself acts in a blind, instinctive way and is in addition fooled by all the illusions that arise when he sees everything that he is not conscious of in himself coming to meet him from outside as projections upon his neighbor. (1945, p. 335)

And finally,

> "Projections change the world into the replica of one's own unknown face" (1955, p. 17)

In "Good and Evil in Analytical Psychology," Jung states:

> To confront a person with his Shadow is to show him his own light. Once one has experienced a few times what it is like to stand judgingly between the opposites, one begins to understand what is meant by the self. Anyone who perceives his Shadow and his light simultaneously sees himself from two sides and thus gets in the middle. (1959, p. 872)

The Self is, according to Jung, the most important archetype. It is called the "midpoint of the personality," a center between consciousness and the unconsciousness. It signifies the harmony and balance between the various opposing qualities that make up the psyche.

The Persona is the mask we wear to make a particular impression on others; it may reveal and conceal our real nature. It is called an artificial personality that is a compromise between a person's real individuality and society's expectations—usually society's demands take precedence. It is made up of things such as professional titles, roles, and habits of social behavior. It serves to both guarantee social order and to protect the individual's private life. That is, when the ego identifies itself with the persona, the individual becomes particularly susceptible to the unconscious.

The Shadow is a step further toward self-realization when one recognizes and integrates it. It is the negative or inferior (underdeveloped) side of the personality. It is said to be made up of all the reprehensible characteristics that each of us wishes to deny. These repressed characteristics of the psyche become dissociated from one's conscious life. The further out of awareness the Shadow is, the blacker and denser it becomes; consequently the greater the need to project its heinous content outward and onto others.

To begin healing, we must invite the shadow self back into awareness—acknowledging its legitimate right to exist and sending a clear message that it will no longer be ignored or rejected. The exercises that follow are designed for that purpose. Bear in mind that shadow work can be triggering, so be sure clients are adequately resourced.

Shadow work can be triggering; prepare appropriately.

Me and My Shadow Exercise

GROUP

Participants should have paper and pencils.

Facilitator gives the following instructions: "Bring to mind a person you don't like very much, possibly even hate. Write down a thorough description of that person, specifically capturing those traits and qualities about this person that you don't like."

Allow everyone in the group enough time to finish.

Instruct the group to now draw a box around what they have written.

Instruct the group to now draw a line on top of the box. On the line, label the box, "MY Shadow."

Facilitator asks the group to consider the following:

"What you have written down is some hidden part of yourself—a part that you have suppressed or concealed. It is what Jung would call your Shadow. It may be a part of you that you fear, can't accept, or hate for some reason. Maybe it's a part of you that needs to be expressed or developed in some way. Maybe you even secretly wish you could be something like that person whom you hate."

Now ask the group to consider the following questions:

- How many of you have or have had friends or romantic partners who fit the description of the "hated" person?
- Is it possible that you may project (or may have projected) those suppressed parts of yourself onto others?
- Isn't it curious how we sometimes choose these "hated" people for our close relationships?

The Imagined House Exercise

GROUP

Often, the house is a symbol of the self, one's own personality. In this guided imagery exercise, participants are instructed to begin to explore a house within their imagination. The processing of this exercise is similar to that of a Gestalt dream interpretation, with questions aimed at what and/or how the house may say something about its own personality (projective identification).

The facilitator should instruct the participants to pay careful attention to all of the details including:

- The house's internal and external appearance
- What can and cannot be found inside the house
- Entrances and exits of the house
- Secret rooms
- Colors, textures, art, and decor
- Participant's internal experience during the house's exploration

The facilitator should read the following script, pausing often to allow time for elaboration and exploration.

MULTISENSORY GUIDED IMAGERY SCRIPT

Begin seeing yourself walking down a road. . . . As you walk, you see a house in the distance. As you move closer, you begin to notice its details. . . . What features stand out? . . . Closer now, you begin to walk around the house, looking at it as you walk. . . . Now you are halfway around. Take particular note of the details of the house as you continue to walk around it. . . . Now you come back to where you were when you started. . . . When you walked around the house, you noticed a way to get in. Go back there and go into the house. . . . What do you see? . . . Explore the house, what's inside? . . . As you are exploring, you notice a secret door leading to a hidden room. Go inside that room. What do you see? . . . Now leave the secret room and go back into the main part of the house. . . . Now go back outside. As you begin walking away from the house, you look back at it one more time, just noticing. . . .

Now you are back on the road once again, walking.

Slowly and gently return to this room, opening your eyes when you feel ready.

Upon completion of the imagery exercise, participants are instructed to write down a detailed description of what they noticed during the exercise, including all sensory information, along with their internal experience and "felt sense" of the house.

The written descriptions are collected, shuffled, and anonymously redistributed.

Each participant then reads to the group the description that (s)he was given.

The facilitator then invites feedback from the group, followed by further discussion or processing as appropriate.

Revealing and Liberating the Shadow:
A Waking Dream Technique

GROUP

Facilitator gives the following instructions:

We are going to meditate briefly on the shadow.

Begin to conjure up your shadow self. Allow it to emerge however it chooses.

With it present, answer the following questions:

- Is it associated with a particular feeling or state?
- Is it linked to a particular place in your body?
- Intensify and stay with those feelings. When did you first experience this during your life?
- Now let the image become separate from your body; allow it stand beside you. How big is it?
- What is it made of?
- What is its connection to your body?

Begin a conversation with the shadow.

- Ask of it its purpose.
- What does it do for you?
- Why did it emerge at that particular time in your life?

Now, allow a spiritual mentor to stand with you and your shadow. Let this mentor fill you with a spiritual peace. Now, allow yourself to absorb all of its wisdom and energy.

Signal your openness, allowing the mentor to:

- Reveal to you the vision of your Higher Self (i.e., you as a completely evolved spiritual being).
- Explain how the shadow will be incorporated into that self.
- Explain the shadow's role in your spiritual evolution.
- Precisely reveal the concrete steps that your evolution will take.

Step into the Higher Self for a few moments and realize the joy, wisdom, humor, love, and opportunities lying in wait for you with this evolution.

Now ask the shadow to merge with the Higher Self. Remind it that the new self fulfills its needs and intentions in every way.

Once the shadow has merged with the Higher Self (possibly not on the first attempt of this exercise) then step into the Higher Self. Reconnect with it—see, hear, feel your connection with it. Wait for a few moments while your Higher Self integrates with your body.

Now, allow it to give you its important spiritual message, which is of concern to you.

Slowly and gently return to this room.

EMOTIONS

Emotions

FYI: NECESSARY DISTINCTIONS

e·mo·tion (*noun*)

the affective aspect of consciousness

a state of feeling

a conscious mental reaction (as anger or fear) subjectively experienced as strong feeling usually directed toward a specific object and typically accompanied by physiological and behavioral changes in the body

af·fect (*noun*)

the conscious subjective aspect of an emotion considered apart from bodily changes; also, a set of observable manifestations of a subjectively experienced emotion

feel·ing (*noun*)

a sensation experienced through this sense

an emotional state or reaction

the overall quality of one's awareness especially as measured along a pleasantness–unpleasantness continuum

Although five competing theories currently explain *how* humans experience emotion, it's probably fair (although arguable) to define *what* humans experience when we use the term, *emotion* as "a feeling state involving physiological changes, thoughts, and an outward expression or behavior."

The next section deals with emotions: how to recognize them, so that we may regulate them.

According to Latner:

> Gestalt therapy is oriented to crucial emotional experiences because they are important to us. An emotion is a focusing of our excitement in such a way that our experiences have meaning. Emotions are the meaning of our experiences. Gestalt therapy encourages experiencing and expressing intense emotions, because they make our existence understandable and satisfying. We must abandon ourselves to them if we are to embrace all of ourselves, and if we are to come to workable solutions. We are not talking here about catharsis, vomiting up emotions to "ventilate" us. "Nature is not so wasteful as to create emotions to throw them away. Emotions are an intrinsic part of experience, and it is necessary for us to recover them in therapy if we are to reorganize our excitement and gratify ourselves. We emphasize the emotional aspect of experience as part of contacting the totality of our lives" [quote attributed to Perls]. (1972, p. 4)

EMOTION LIST		
absorbed	controlling	perfectionistic
abusive	courageous	possessive
accepting	critical	punishing
accommodating	cruel	rejecting
accomplished	curious	resentful
activated	defeated	resigned
adversarial	deluded	resistant
aggressive	demanding	responsible
agreeable	dependent	ridiculous
alert	depressed	righteous
altruistic	insecure	ruthless
angry	insensitive	sad
annoyed	inspired	sadistic
anxious	interested	secretive
arrogant	intolerant	selfish
ashamed	introspective	self-sabotaging
authentic	irresponsible	sensitive
balanced	irritable	serene
beautiful	irritated	shamed
belligerent	isolated	shut-down
bereft	jealous	shy
bitter	joyful	sorry
bored	judged	stimulated
brave	judgmental	stricken
broken down	lazy	strung-out
bullied	lonely	stubborn
calm	lost	superior
chaotic	loved	suspicious
cheerful	loving	tolerant
cold	manipulated	understanding
commanding	manipulative	unforgiving
compassionate	miserable	vain
competitive	mistrusting	vicious
complaining	negative	victimized
conceited	obsessed	violent
condemned	open	wise
confident	overly responsible	withdrawn
conflicted	panicky	worried
confused	paranoid	worthy
content	passionate	
controlled	passive	

EMOTION PROFILE

1. List some things that tend to make you angry:

_____

_____

_____

_____

2. List some things that make you feel sad:

_____

_____

_____

_____

3. List some things that make you feel guilty:

_____

_____

_____

_____

4. List some things that make you feel shame:

_____

_____

_____

_____

5. List some things that make you feel happy or joyous:

_____

_____

_____

_____

6. List some things that make you feel scared:

_____

_____

_____

_____

7. List some things that make you feel fulfilled or satisfied:

_____

_____

_____

_____

8. List some things that make you feel discouraged:

_____

_____

_____

_____

9. With which of these emotions are you most familiar?

_____

_____

_____

_____

10. With which emotions are you most unfamiliar?

_____

_____

_____

_____

Consider your answers to #9 and #10. What would you like to change in these answers?

Exploding Water Balloons: Releasing Anger

GROUP

MATERIALS:

- Water balloons (at least three/participants) and tap connector
  - Balloon 200 pc *water bomb w/nozzle* by **unique** $5.49
  - Water balloons with nozzle and knotter and 250 bonus balloons by *Tie-Not Inc.* $3.99
- Indelible markers
- Plastic bags (e.g., trashcan liners or grocery store bags)
- Brick wall (preferably outside)

INSTRUCTIONS:

Ask participants to bring to mind an instance when they felt really angry—*just think about it; don't talk about it yet.* (This instance could be an isolated incident, a particular person, or an amalgam of many interactions.)

Ask participants to recall two additional incidents when they felt really angry—*just think about them; don't talk about them yet.* (They could be isolated incidents, a particular person, or an amalgam of many interactions.)

Confirm that all participants were able to come up with three instances, and then instruct each participant to line up to fill their balloons with water.

Have participants return to their seats and dry the excess water from the exterior of the balloons. Then, they may use the marker to write one or two words that capture the provoking incident/person/relationship onto one of the balloons. Repeat with the other two balloons.

Once completed, each participant should put his/her three balloons into his/her plastic bag; then, the group is lead outside to the brick wall.

Instruct the group to line up in front of the wall, as each participant will be throwing his/her balloons against it.

Each participant should:

1. Choose the first of the three labeled balloons.
2. Reconnect to the feelings of anger.
3. Embody those emotions.
4. With full awareness of thoughts, emotions, and body sensations, release the balloon, along with the accompanying anger and energy.

Allow each participant his/her three throws.

Facilitate discussion regarding entire process, from beginning to end.

Pick up the remains of the exploded balloons.

Fear Fantasy

GROUP

INSTRUCTIONS:

The group facilitator will lead the group in a guided imagery exercise.

"We will begin by having you close your eyes or focus on a spot a foot or two in front of you where you will not be distracted. Now imagine or fantasize about an extreme situation in which you are faced with your own specific fear. Once you have induced a vivid scene in fantasy, notice as you begin to feel the fear. . . .

The facilitator now asks the following questions:

- How do you know when you are afraid?
- What bodily changes do you experience?
- Which comes first, the awareness in your mind or the bodily changes?
- Now, paying attention to each of your senses, notice:
  - How does your fear feel?
  - How does your fear taste?
  - How does your fear smell?
  - How does your fear look?
  - How does your fear sound?

The facilitator instructs the group members to breathe deeply and gently open their eyes . . . returning to this room. The facilitator next asks the group to notice any thoughts, feelings, or sensations.

When everyone is present and oriented to place and time, the discussion begins. The facilitator begins by asking for process comments.

What was that like for you? What did you notice? Was anything surprising to you?

According to William James: "Action seems to follow feeling but really action and feeling go together; and by regulating the action, which is under the more direct control of the will, we can indirectly regulate the feeling, which is not" (http://www.uky.edu/~eushe2/Pajares/jgospel.html).

In *The Expression of the Emotions in Man and Animals*, Charles Darwin wrote:

The free expression by outward signs of an emotion intensifies it. On the other hand, the repression, as far as this is possible, of all outward signs softens our emotions. . . . Even the simulation of an emotion tends to arouse it in our minds." (2009)

The "facial feedback" (theory of emotion) posits that physically expressing an emotion sends a biochemical signal from the facial muscles that "loops" back to the brain (e.g., sound emanating from a speaker is picked up by a microphone and looped back through a speaker as amplified feedback). Empirical studies lend support to the theory, demonstrating that emotions stimulate physical expressions, and physical expressions stimulate emotions.

This facial feedback mechanism works both individually and in groups. (Remember mirror neurons?) Anecdotally, we know that seeing or hearing others laugh tends to make us laugh, which in turn makes them laugh more, which in turn makes us laugh more. Basically, when we are in a group of laughing people we are part of a powerful servo system—an assemblage of internal and external feedback loops of positive emotion.

> **It seems that improving emotion regulation through conscious control may be easier than once thought. The exercises that follow will assist in the up-regulation of positive emotion.**

Facial expressions are a hardwired part of emotions. In primitive societies and among animals, facial expressions communicate like words. Even in modern societies, facial expressions communicate faster than words. Regardless of whether we intend it, the communication of emotions influences others. The forward and backward action of the jaw is primarily related to the lip reaching and smiling functions of the face. All primates need the social gestures of the face and jaw to survive in their community. Even though these actions are not necessary to chew food, they are important social gestures that promote survival of an individual within the community; therefore, you might think of these forward and backward motions of the jaw and face as *social movements*.

Positive Emotion

DEVELOPING A MORE EXPRESSIVE FACE
INDIVIDUAL OR GROUP

Our expression and our words never coincide, which is why the animals don't understand us.

~Malcolm de Chazal

This lesson will reveal how the muscles of the face act in harmony with the actions of the jaw. If the muscles of the lips, the cheeks, and the rest of our face do not move, it is more difficult for the jaw to move freely.

INSTRUCTIONS:

Begin the exercise lying on the floor on your back. Once you've practiced for a while, repeat while sitting upright in a chair.

Lie on your back in a comfortable position, with your back, neck, and spine fully supported. Knowing that you will not be interrupted for the next little while, begin by gently closing your eyes.

1. Now begin to bring your attention to your breath—the direct experience of your breath—however it is . . . and however it changes. Allow yourself to softly focus your awareness onto the breath that is arising right now . . . the in-breath and the out-breath . . . the rising and the falling. If you can, try to follow one full cycle of the breath from the beginning of the in-breath and through its entirety to the beginning of the out-breath and through its entirety. Allow yourself the time and the space to be in direct contact with the breath throughout one entire cycle.

2. Place both your index and middle fingers just below your ears, locating the hinge of the jaw. Keeping your eyes lightly closed, begin to gently open and close your jaw; slide the jaw side to side as well. Bring your attention to how the movement feels under your fingers.

3. Now, gently glide your jaw forward and backward
   - Do you feel more strain in your throat or neck while doing this movement?
   - Can you facilitate the gliding movement with your lips?

4. Stop the movement of the jaw, and take your lips forward and back.
   - How does that affect your jaw?

5. Purse or pucker your lips as if you were going to kiss someone.
   - Do you notice how your jaw automatically glides forward?

6. Now, slowly pull your lips back into an enormous grin.

- Do you notice that when you begin to smile that your jaw retracts? (The bigger the smile, the greater the motion of the jaw.)
- Can you feel your jaw gliding backward?

7. Alternate between puckering your lips and grinning widely, noticing the feeling in your jaw as it glides forward and back with the movement of your lips.
   - Notice whether your neck also participates in this forward and backward movement.

8. After you have mastered the slow movement of the lips, jaw, and head, increase the speed and fluidity of the movement.

9. Try turning your head to either side, and then perform the same movement while aiming in a different direction.

10. Rest.

Exercises from the World of Positive Psychology

GROUP OR INDIVIDUAL

These exercises were designed to increase overall happiness and a sense of well-being, and both have been empirically proven to do so. Not surprisingly, both come compliments of my hometown's *happiness expert*, the director of Positive Psychology Center at the University of Pennsylvania, a.k.a. the "Father of Positive Psychology," Martin Seligman. (Applause understood.)

Due to the evolutionary process, it seems that the human brain developed a strong tendency to ignore what goes well in life and to selectively focus on what might go wrong. Granted, this tendency was an extremely effective survival strategy back in the day when humans were considered a nutritious food source by many other species.

Even though our environment has changed considerably, the human brain has not yet relinquished its negative bias. We remain hardwired to process the negative, while downplaying the positive. To combat this tendency, in the service of nourishing our well-being, we humans must *actively* develop a more optimistic outlook, which requires us to *intentionally focus attention* on our positive experiences and then to *consciously savor and relish them*. Seligman and others have devised and used these three simple techniques to do just that.

Three Blessings

(Adapted from Seligman.)

INSTRUCTIONS:

Every night for the next week, just before you go to bed, think about anything good that happened to you during that day. Write down three of these things.

Remember exactly how each good thing happened, then—even more important—think about *why* each thing happened. Make a point to recognize the giver behind the gift (i.e., think about the person who made this pleasant thing happen). For example, maybe a coworker brought you a cup of coffee or a friend called just to check in. Maybe somebody held the door for you or let you merge into traffic. Maybe you witnessed an act of kindness. It doesn't matter whether the experience was big or small. Bring it to mind: relish your good fortune or savor the kindness. It's been shown that the longer one holds an emotionally charged event in his/her awareness, the stronger its trace in memory (Lewis, 2005).

1. *What*: One good thing that happened today:

   _____

   _____

   _____

   _____

2. *How*: It happened like this:

   _____

   _____

   _____

   _____

3. *Why*: It happened because:

   _____

   _____

   _____

Taking In the Good

(Adapted from Seligman.)

INSTRUCTIONS:

Relax and, if you like, gently close your eyes. As vividly as possible, bring to mind the feeling of any of the positive emotions that you experienced today. Once you've chosen one, begin to intensify these feelings and sensations. Try to remember, or if you can't remember, just imagine what may have made these emotions feel so strong for you today.

Remain with the sense of these positive emotions. . . . Experience the bodily sensations that accompany them. Pay specific attention to the area around your heart, face, and stomach. Whether the sensations are mild or intense, just notice them . . . experience them.

Now, sense that these positive feelings are beginning to sink deeply into you . . . notice any sensations that may be settling into your back . . . or any other part of your body. . . . Notice as they are becoming a part of you . . . growing and becoming part of your inner landscape . . . breathing into those places and continuing to sense these positive emotions sinking into yourself.

Gratitude Letter

(Adapted from Seligman.)

By writing someone a letter of gratitude and reading it aloud to him/her, you can experience firsthand the benefits of gratitude.

INSTRUCTIONS:

Write a letter to someone you appreciate, perhaps someone who has made a difference in your life and to whom you feel grateful. Choose a benefactor—someone who has contributed to your life in a meaningful way. Take as long as you need to write this letter, there is no time limit. . . . Once satisfied with your letter, send it the person, or, if possible, arrange to meet with this person and read the letter to him/her.

Think about some ways that (s)he has contributed to you and has had positive effects on your life.

- Write down *general* and *specific* things that this person has done for you and how his/her actions have affected your life, including how (s)he made you feel.
- If meeting is a possibility, do not tell the person about the letter beforehand.
- When you meet, read your letter aloud to him/her.
- Allow the person time and space for your message of gratitude to be absorbed.
- Try to remain attuned to your own reactions, emotions, thoughts, and sensations that come up as you read the letter.

Spend time afterward reflecting with this person on the effects of the letter and the impact that (s)he has had on your life.

Regardless of whether forgiveness is a worthy virtue, a moral duty or something altogether different, in psychological studies, it happens that forgiveness is closely correlated with increased happiness and improved mental health. It seems that most of us would welcome happiness and better mental health. Right? Well, like everything else, that would depend on the personal cost involved:

- Am I required to condone the behavior of the perpetrator?
- Does it mean that the behavior was okay? (I should put up with it, because there was no *real injury*.)
- Must I develop selective amnesia and simply forget all about it . . . or at least pretend to?
- Must I pardon this person—allowing him/her to continue causing more damage?
- Must I reconcile with this person? Or get back into a relationship, where I'll get hurt all over again?

NO. The answer is no to all of them.

The quintessential nature of forgiveness: it is *a voluntary decision to acknowledge the offense, move through the resultant feelings, set aside the resentment, and release the anger, so you may move on with your life*. You **need not** condone, excuse, forget, or reestablish a relationship with the perpetrator.

Pardoning: It is problematic when forgiveness is coupled with, or equated to, pardoning. Freedman and Enright (1996) believe that a person can forgive, yet still expect justice. As they view forgiveness and justice to be in harmony with each other—both inviting and provoking change and growth.

Condoning: Forgiving the perpetrator for his/her action(s) does not mean you stop judging the deed. You forgive the person, not the action. Forgiveness allows you to live in the present and leave the past behind. Forgiveness will bring you peace. Freedman and Enright (1996) posit that condoning denies the resentment and the offense, which is likely to exacerbate and complicate the hurt and injury. In contrast to denial, forgiveness vanquishes the resentment with love and compassion.

"Resentment is like taking poison and hoping the other person dies."

~Augustine of Hippo

Reconciliation: It is possible to accept, even love a person and still choose not to be in a personal relationship with him or her. Aponte states, "Reconciliation is distinct from the moral decision to forgive. The choice to forgive [only] opens the door . . . to reconciliation, if **safe, prudent, and right**." In contrast to the notion that forgiveness be offered by the offended person, Freedman and Enright (1996) believe that reconciliation is the offender's responsibility and occurs when the offender recognizes his/her wrong and takes actions to correct the offending behavior. Further, forgiveness may take place when the offended gives up feelings of hatred or resentment, but does not necessarily restore the relationship with the offender.

FORGIVENESS: MYTH BUSTING
EXERCISE:

This experiential format can be used to address the modern myths and misconceptions around the concept of forgiveness.

INSTRUCTIONS:

1. Print, distribute, and have participants read the worksheet, **Forgiveness: What It Is . . . and Isn't.**

2. Write each of the following myths on separate pages.
   - *If I forgive this person, it means that I'm condoning the behavior of the person I'm forgiving.*
   - *If I forgive this person, then my relationship with him/her will certainly improve.*
   - *If I forgive this person, then I won't be angry about what happened.*
   - *If I forgive, I give up my right to feel hurt, angry, or sad.*
   - *I haven't really forgiven that person when I remember what happened.*
   - *I should only have to forgive once (i.e., once I do it, I'll never have to think about it again).*
   - *I forgive, not for me, but for the sake of the other person.*
   - *If I forgive this person, I must remain in a relationship with this person.*

3. Read each myth aloud; then place the page on the floor, announcing to the group that this area is now dedicated to that myth.

4. Invite each participant to walk around the room, to reread each one.

5. Once read, (s)he should then choose the one (s)he feels the most energy around or the most identification with and stand in that designated area.

6. Once all of the participants are in a designated area, begin with the least populated area and invite each group member in it to share:
   - Why (s)he chose the one that (s)he did.
   - How (s)he identifies with the myth.

7. Moving on to the next group, repeat the process for each myth.

8. After everyone has spoken, have participants return to their seats.

9. Process the experience in a *go-round*, allowing participants to share thoughts and feelings regarding any aspect of the exercise and/or any aspect of forgiveness itself.

WORKSHEET: STAGES OF FORGIVENESS

STAGE ONE: IDENTIFY PERPETRATOR AND TRANSGRESSION

- I know who it was that has affected me negatively.
- I know what specific behavior(s) it was that has been physically, emotionally, or spiritually damaging to me.

STAGE TWO: IDENTIFY, EXPERIENCE, AND PROCESS THE EMOTIONS

- I have felt the emotions associated with the offensive, damaging behavior. I have found a safe place to process these feelings.
- If it was safe to do so, I have spoken to the person regarding the adverse effects I endured as a result of his/her behavior.
- If it was not safe to do so, I was able to do it in therapy using an imaginary technique (e.g., role playing, psychodrama, the empty chair, etc.).

STAGE THREE: UNDERSTAND THE NEED FOR FORGIVENESS

- I understand the benefits of forgiveness (see Worksheet: *Forgiveness: Why Should I?*)
- I have reached a point where I recognize what has transpired, have begun developing compassion for myself, and am now able to see the perpetrator as a human being.

Important Distinction: Many people, including clergy members, philosophers, psychotherapists, and psychologists, *erroneously* believe that full forgiveness requires the victim to accept the perpetrator back into the relationship. What is actually required of the victim is that (s)he accept the perpetrator back into the human race (i.e., (s)he is no longer stripped of his/her humanity, regardless of whether the victim chooses to reestablish a personal relationship with him/her).

As Joan Borysenko states in *Guilt Is the Teacher, Love Is the Lesson*

Forgiveness is not a lack of discrimination whereby we let all the criminals out of prison: it is an attitude that permits us to relate to the pain that led to their errors and recognize their need for love. (1991, p. XXX)

STAGE FOUR: SET CLEAR BOUNDARIES

- I have set clear boundaries with the perpetrator:
- I understand the need for and my right to protect myself.
- I feel competent in setting and maintaining these boundaries to keep me physically and emotionally safe.

STAGE FIVE: INTEGRATE THE PAST AND BEGIN RECREATING THE FUTURE

- I have made an internal choice to forgive and a have willingness to recreate a meaningful life for myself.

Stages of Forgiveness

EXERCISE:

This experiential format helps in understanding forgiveness as a stage model, similar to the stages of grief.

INSTRUCTIONS:

1. Invite each participant to choose a forgiveness issue that (s)he is currently dealing with, or is considering dealing with.
2. Print, distribute, and have participants read the worksheet, *The Stages of Forgiveness*. Print the following pages. Each page contains one of the stages of forgiveness:

STAGE ONE: IDENTIFY THE PERPETRATOR AND THE TRANSGRESSION

- I know who it was that has affected me negatively.
- I know what specific behavior(s) it was that has been physically, emotionally, or spiritually damaging to me.

STAGE TWO: IDENTIFY, EXPERIENCE, AND PROCESS THE EMOTIONS

- I have felt the emotions associated with the offensive, damaging behavior. I have found a safe place to process these feelings.
- If it was safe to do so, I have spoken to the person regarding the adverse effects I endured as a result of his/her behavior.
- If it was not safe to do so, I was able to do it in therapy using an imaginary technique (e.g., role playing, psychodrama, the empty chair, etc.).

STAGE THREE: UNDERSTAND THE NEED FOR FORGIVENESS

- I understand the benefits of forgiveness.
- I have reached a point where I recognize what has transpired, have begun developing compassion for myself, and am now able to see the perpetrator as a human being.

STAGE FOUR: SET CLEAR BOUNDARIES

- I have set clear boundaries with the perpetrator:
- I understand my need and my right to protect myself.
- I feel competent in setting and maintaining these boundaries to keep me physically and emotionally safe.

STAGE FIVE: INTEGRATE THE PAST AND BEGIN RECREATING THE FUTURE

- I have made an internal choice to forgive and have a willingness to recreate a meaningful life for myself.

4. Read each stage aloud; then place the corresponding page onto the floor.

5. Invite each participant to walk around the room, to reread each one.

6. Once read, with regard to his/her perpetrator, the participant should then choose the stage that (s)he feels (s)he is in presently.

7. Once all of the participants are in a designated area, ask the question, "Why have you chosen this stage?" Invite them to think about the answer.

8. After a few moments of reflection, instruct participants to walk to the area designated to the next stage (e.g., if participant is standing at Stage One, then move to Stage Two, if standing in Stage Three, then move to Stage Four, etc.).

9. Once all participants have moved, ask these questions:
   - Could you foresee yourself moving onto the next stage in reality?
   - If so, what would need to happen for you to do that?

10. Invite them to think about their answer(s).

11. Invite participants to return to their seats.

12. Process the experience in two *go-rounds:*
   - First *go-round:* Invite participants to share their answer to one or both questions.
   - Second *go-round:* Invite participants to share thoughts and feelings regarding any aspect of the exercise and/or any aspect of the stages of forgiveness.

Stage One

IDENTIFY PERPETRATOR AND TRANSGRESSION

I know who it was that has affected me negatively.

I know what specific behavior(s) it was that has been physically, emotionally or spiritually damaging to me.

Stage Two

IDENTIFY, EXPERIENCE, AND PROCESS THE EMOTIONS

• I have felt the emotions associated with the offensive, damaging behavior. I have found a safe place process these feelings.

• If it was safe to do so, I have spoken to the person regarding the adverse effects I endured as a result of his/her behavior.

• If it was not safe to do so, I was able to do it in therapy using an imaginary technique (e.g., role playing, psychodrama, the empty chair, etc.).

Stage Three

UNDERSTAND THE NEED FOR FORGIVENESS

• I understand the benefits of forgiveness.

• I have reached a point where I recognize what has transpired, have begun developing compassion for myself, and am now able to see the perpetrator as a human being.

Stage Four

SET CLEAR BOUNDARIES

- I have set clear boundaries with the perpetrator:

- I understand the need for and my right to protect myself.

- I feel competent in setting and maintaining these boundaries to keep me physically and emotionally safe.

Stage Five

I have made an internal choice to forgive and have willingness to recreate a meaningful life for myself.

WORKSHEET: CRISIS TO-DO LIST

Breathe: Take a few deep breaths, and mindfully observe the breath flowing in and flowing out.

Notice: Take note of your experience in this moment. Notice what you are thinking, feeling, and doing. Allow room for each feeling. Open up to each thought as well, without clinging or holding onto any of them. Remind yourself that there can be space.

Right now I am thinking:

_____

_____

_____

_____

Right now I feel:

_____

_____

_____

_____

Breathe into each feeling, allowing each the required space. Without pushing them away, remind yourself that they—like everything else—are transient. Allow them to move through you . . . observing them, without becoming them.

Once you've given space to the thoughts and feelings, begin the inquiry:

How do I want to be in the face of this crisis?

_____

_____

_____

_____

What values matter here?

_____

_____

_____

How would I like to behave?

_____

_____

_____

Do I need some help? Or advice?

_____

_____

_____

Who can I call on for support or assistance in this situation?

_____

_____

_____

Has something like this happened before? If so, what did I do?

_____

_____

_____

What did I learn that might help now?

_____

_____

_____

Was that action or reaction helpful
. . . in the short and long term?

_____

_____

_____

_____

. . . in the next half hour?

_____

_____

_____

_____

. . . in the next few hours?

_____

_____

_____

_____

. . . in the next few days?

_____

_____

_____

_____

If truly nothing can be done to improve the situation, am I willing to practice some acceptance skills?

Given the givens: What's the most constructive thing I can do here?

_____

_____

_____

_____

What can I learn from this situation?

_____

_____

_____

_____

How can I grow from this experience?

_____

_____

_____

_____

One final question: "If someone whom I love and care about was in this same situation, (thoughts and feeling included), how would I act toward him/her?"

_____

_____

_____

_____

What things would I say?

_____

_____

_____

_____

What advice might I give?

_____

_____

_____

_____

Is it possible to act "as if" you were that person who deserves that type of love,
compassion, and support?

Reference / Additional Reading

Amen, D.

- *Change Your Brain, Change Your Body: Use Your Brain to Get and Keep the Body You Have Always Wanted.* New York: Three Rivers Press, 2010.

Aponte, H.

- "Political Bias, Moral Values, and Spirituality in the Training of Psychotherapists." *Bulletin of the Menninger Clinic* 60 (1996): 488–502.

Blatner, A.

- *Acting-In: Practical Applications of Psychodramatic Methods.* New York: Springer Publishing Company, 1996.

Brisch, K. H.

- *Treating Attachment Disorders: From Theory to Therapy.* New York: The Guilford Press, 2004.

Calais-Germain, B.

- *Anatomy of Movement.* Seattle, WA: Eastland Press, 2007.

Carbonell, J. and Figley, C. R.

- "The Systematic Clinical Demonstration: Methodology for the Initial Examination of Clinical Innovations." *Traumatology* 2.1 (1996). Retrieved from www.fsu.edu/~trauma.

Carter, C. S., Ahnert, L., Grossmann, K. E., Hrdy, S. B., Lamb, M., Porges, S., and Sachser, N.

- *Attachment and Bonding: A New Synthesis.* Boston: The MIT Press, 2005.

Cornell, A.W.

- *Power of Focusing: A Practical Guide to Emotional Self-Healing.* Oakland, CA: New Harbinger Publications, 1996.
- "The Focusing Institute." In *Carrying Life Forward Through Thought,* 2012. Retrieved from http://www.focusing.org (November 20, 2012).

Craig, G.

- *EFT Emotional Freedom Techniques for PTSD (Post-Traumatic Stress Disorder).* Fulton, CA: Energy Psychology Press, 2008.

Curran, L.

- *Trauma Treatment: Psychotherapy for the 21st Century: Mistakes Made, Lessons Learned.* Eau Claire, WI: PESI Publishing and Media, 2012.

Darwin, C. and Eckman, P.

- *The Expression of the Emotions in Man and Animals,* 4th ed. New York: Oxford University Press, 2009.

Dayton, T.

- *The Drama Within: Psychodrama and Experiential Therapy*. Deerfield Beach, FL: HCI, 1994.
- *Trauma and Addiction: Ending the Cycle of Pain Through Emotional Literacy*. Deerfield Beach, FL: HCI, 2000.
- *Diagnostic and Statistical Manual of Mental Disorders*, 4th ed., text revision (DSM-IV-TR). American Psychiatric Association, 2000.

Dowrick, S.

- *Creative Journal Writing: The Art and Heart of Reflection*. Los Angeles: Tarcher, 2009.

Eden, D.

- *Energy Medicine: Balancing Your Body's Energies for Optimal Health, Joy, and Vitality*. Los Angeles: Tarcher, 2008.

Emerson, D. and Hopper, E.

- *Overcoming Trauma through Yoga: Reclaiming Your Body*. Berkeley, CA: North Atlantic Books, 2011.

Emerson, D., Sharma, R., Chaudry, S., and Turner, J.

- "Trauma-Sensitive Yoga Therapy in Practice: Trauma-Sensitive Yoga: Principles, Practice, and Research." *International Journal of Yoga Therapy* 19 (2009): 123–128.

Engel, B.

- *Healing Your Emotional Self: A Powerful Program to Help You Raise Your Self-Esteem, Quiet Your Inner Critic, and Overcome Your Shame*. New York: Wiley, 2007.

Enright, R.D., Enright, S., and The Human Development Study Group

- "Counseling within the Forgiveness Triad: On Forgiving, Receiving Forgiveness, and Self-Forgiveness." *Counseling and Values* 40 (1996): 107–126.

Fagan, J. and Shepherd, I. L. (eds.)

- *Gestalt Therapy Now*. New York: Harper, 1970/1971.

Feldenkrais, M.

- *Awareness Through Movement: Easy-to-Do Health Exercises to Improve Your Posture, Vision, Imagination, and Personal Awareness*. New York: HarperOne, 1991.

Fonagy, F.

- *Affect Regulation, Mentalization, and the Development of Self*. New York: Other Press, 2005.

Forbes, B.

- *Yoga for Emotional Balance: Simple Practices to Help Relieve Anxiety and Depression*. Boston: Shambhala, 2011.

Forrest, A.

- *Fierce Medicine: Breakthrough Practices to Heal the Body and Ignite the Spirit*. New York: HarperOne, 2011.

Gendlin, E.

- *Focusing.* New York: Bantam Books, 1982.
- *Focusing-Oriented Psychotherapy: A Manual of the Experiential Method.* New York: The Guilford Press, 1998.

Gershoni, J.

- *Psychodrama in the 21st Century: Clinical and Educational Applications.* New York: Springer, 2003.

Goldenberg, H, Goldenberg, I.

- Family Therapy: An Overview, Brooks Cole; 8th edition, 2012

Hahn, T. N.

- *Reconciliation: Healing the Inner Child.* Berkeley, CA: Parallax Press, 2010.

Herman, J.

- *Trauma and Recovery: The Aftermath of Violence—from Domestic Abuse to Political Terror.* New York: Basic Books, 1997.

Iacoboni, M.

- *Mirroring People: The Science of Empathy and How We Connect with Others.* New York: Picador, 2009.

James, W.,

- *The Gospel of Relaxation.* University of Kentucky, 2008. Retrieved from http://www.uky.edu/~eushe2/Pajares/jgospel.html (November 20, 2012).

Jung, C. G.

- *The Archetypes and The Collective Unconscious (Collected Works of C.G. Jung Vol.9 Part 1)* Princeton: Princeton University Press, 1970.
- *Civilization in Transition (Collected Works of C.G. Jung Vol.10).* Princeton: Princeton University Press, 1970.
- *Good and Evil in Analytical Psychology"* (1959). *(Collected Works of C.G. Jung Vol.10).* Princeton: Princeton University Press, 1970.
- "The Philosophical Tree" (1945). In CW 13: *Alchemical Studies. (Collected Works of C.G. Jung Vol.10).* Princeton: Princeton University Press, 1970.

Kabat-Zinn, J.

- *Full Catastrophe Living: Using the Wisdom of Your Body and Mind to Face Stress, Pain, and Illness.* McHenry, IL: Delta, 1990.

Kaminoff, L. and Matthews, A.

- *Yoga Anatomy*, 2nd ed. Champaign, IL: Human Kinetics, 2011.

Karen, R.

- *Becoming Attached: First Relationships and How They Shape our Capacity to Love.* New York: Oxford University Press, 1998.

Karp, M., Holmes, P., and Bradshaw, K. Tauvon (eds.)

- *The Handbook of Psychodrama.* New York: Routledge, 1998.

Kellermann, P.

- *Focus on Psychodrama: The Therapeutic Aspects of Psychodrama*. London: Jessica Kingsley, 1992.

- *Psychodrama with Trauma Survivors: Acting Out Your Pain*. London: Jessica Kingsley, 2000.

Kirchner, M.

- "Gestalt Therapy Theory: An Overview." *Gestalt!* 3.4 (2000). Retrieved from http://www.g-gej.org/4-3/theoryoverview.html.

Koch, L.

- *The Psoas Book*. Felton, CA: Guinea Pig Publications, 2012.

Kraftsow, G.

- *Viniyoga Therapy for Anxiety for Beginners to Advanced,* with Gary Kraftsow (DVD) 2011.

Kushi, M.

- *The Book of Do-In: Exercise for Physical and Spiritual Development*. Tokyo: Japan Publications, 1979.

Latner, J.

- *The Gestalt Therapy Book: A Holistic Guide to the Theory, Principles, and Techniques of Gestalt Therapy Developed by Frederick S. Perls and Others*. Gouldsboro, ME: The Gestalt Journal Press, 1972/1989.

Levine, P.

- *Healing Trauma: A Pioneering Program for Restoring the Wisdom of Your Body* Sounds True Inc. (2005).

- *Waking the Tiger: Healing Trauma: The Innate Capacity to Transform Overwhelming Experiences*. Berkeley, CA: North Atlantic Books, 1997.

- *In an Unspoken Voice: How the Body Releases Trauma and Restores Goodness*. Berkeley, CA: North Atlantic Books, 2010.

Lewis, K., Lange, D., and Gillis, L.

- "Transactive Memory Systems, Learning, and Learning Transfer." *Organization Science* 16 (November/December 2005):581–598.

Long, R.

- *The Key Muscles of Yoga: Scientific Keys*. Baldwinsville, NY: BandhaYoga, 2009.

- *The Key Poses of Yoga: Scientific Keys, Vol. II*. Baldwinsville, NY: BandhaYoga, 2009.

Lusk, J.

- *30 Scripts for Relaxation, Imagery & Inner Healing*, Vol. 2. Duluth, MN: Whole Person Associates, 1993.

Naparstek, B.

- *Invisible Heroes: Survivors of Trauma and How They Heal*. New York: Bantam, 2004.

- *Staying Well With Guided Imagery*. New York: Grand Central Publishing, 1995.

Naranjo, C.

- *Gestalt Therapy: The Attitude and Practice of an Atheoretical Experientialism*, Crown House Publishing, 2000

- *The Way of Silence and the Talking Cure: On Meditation and Psychotherapy*, Blue Dolphin Publishing, Inc, 2006

Parnell, L:

- A Therapist's Guide to EMDR: Tools and Techniques for Successful Treatment W. W. Norton & Company; (2006)

- Tapping In: A Step-by-Step Guide to Activating Your Healing Resources Through Bilateral Stimulation W. W. Norton & Company; (2007)

Perls, F.

- "Dream Seminars." In J. Fagan and I. L. Shepherd (eds.). *Gestalt Therapy Now*. New York: Harper & Row, 1970.

Perls, F., Hefferline, R., and Goodman, P.

- *Gestalt Therapy: Excitement and Growth in the Human Personality*, rev. ed. Gouldsboro, ME: Gestalt Journal Press, 1951/1994.

Pert, C.

- *Molecules of Emotion: The Science Behind Mind-Body Medicine*. New York: Simon & Schuster, 1999.

Polster, E. and Polster, M.

- *The Heart of Gestalt Therapy* (Gestalt Institute of Cleveland Press Book Series). Gouldsboro, ME: Gestalt Journal Press, 2000.

Porges, S.

- *The Polyvagal Theory: Neurophysiological Foundations of Emotions, Attachment, Communication, and Self-regulation*. New York: W. W. Norton & Company, 2011.

- *The polyvagal theory: New insights into adaptive reactions of the autonomic nervous system.* Cleveland Clinic Journal of Medicine, 76:S86-90. 2009

- "Music Therapy and Trauma: Insights from the Polyvagal Theory." In K Stewart (ed.), *Symposium on Music Therapy & Trauma: Bridging Theory and Clinical Practice* (pp. 3–15). New York: Satchnote Press, 2010.

Ray, R.

- *Your Breathing Body*, Vol. 1. Louisville, CO: Sounds True, 2008.

Rothschild, B.

- *The Body Remembers: The Psychophysiology of Trauma and Trauma Treatment*, W. W. Norton & Company, 2000.

- *The Body Remembers Casebook: Unifying Methods and Models in the Treatment of Trauma and PTSD*, W. W. Norton & Company, 2003.

- *8 Keys to Safe Trauma Recovery: Take-Charge Strategies to Empower Your Healing*, W. W. Norton & Company, 2010.

- *Help for the Helper: The Psychophysiology of Compassion Fatigue and Vicarious Trauma*, W. W. Norton & Company, 2006.

- *Trauma Essentials: The Go-To Guide (Go-To Guides)*, W. W. Norton & Company, 2011.

Savard, M.

- *Critical Collaboration: Adlerian Therapy and Gestalt Therapy.* Ann Arbor, MI: ProQuest, UMI Dissertation Publishing, 2011.

Salzberg, S.

- *Real Happiness: The Power of Meditation: A 28-Day Program.* New York: Workman Publishing Company, 2010.

Scaer, RC.

- *The Body Bears the Burden: Trauma, Dissociation, and Disease,* The Haworth Press; 2 edition, 2007.
- *The Trauma Spectrum: Hidden Wounds and Human Resiliency,* The Haworth Press; 2005.

Schore, A.

- *Affect Regulation and the Origin of the Self.* New York: W. W. Norton & Company, 1994.

Schwartz. A.

- *Guided Imagery for Groups: Fifty Visualizations That Promote Relaxation, Problem-Solving, Creativity, and Well-Being.* Duluth, MN: Whole Person Associates, 1995.

Shapiro, R:

- EMDR Solutions: Pathways to Healing W. W. Norton & Company, 2005.
- *EMDR Solutions II: For Depression, Eating Disorders, Performance, and More,* W. W. Norton & Company, 2009.

Siegel, D. J.

- *Healing Trauma: Attachment, Mind, Body, and Brain,* W. W. Norton & Company, 2003.
- *The Mindful Therapist: A Clinician's Guide to Mindsight and Neural Integration.* Norton Series on Interpersonal Neurobiology, 2010.
- *Mindsight: The New Science of Personal Transformation.* New York: Bantam Books, 2011.

Suler, J.

- "Zen Stories to Tell Your Neighbors." In *Zen Stories to Tell Your Neighbors.* 2012. Retrieved from http://users.rider.edu/~suler/zenstory/zenstory.html (November 20, 2012).

Tulku, T.

- *Tibetan Meditation.* London: Duncan Baird, 2006.

van der Kolk, B.

- *Traumatic Stress: The Effects of Overwhelming Experience on Mind, Body, and Society.* New York: The Guilford Press, 2006.

Weintraub, A.

- *Yoga Skills for Therapists: Effective Practices for Mood Management.* New York: W. W. Norton & Company, 2012.

Wildman, F.

- *Feldenkrais: The Busy Person's Guide to Easier Movement.* Berkeley, CA: The Intelligent Body Press, 2006.

Wilkins, P.

- *Psychodrama* (Creative Therapies in Practice series). Thousand Oaks, CA: Sage Publications, 1999.

Wilson, S.

- *Qi Gong for Beginners: Eight Easy Movements for Vibrant Health.* New York: Sterling, 2007.

Winnicott, D.

- "Transitional Objects and Transitional Phenomena." *International Journal of Psychoanalysis* 34 (1953): 89–97.

Made in the USA
Middletown, DE
12 February 2020